MIND-FUL CONSULTING

To dear Angela
Here's to a mindful
continuing connection

Karen

MIND-FUL
CONSULTING

edited by
Sue Whittle and Karen Izod

Angela —
Grave to have your
support.
Best wishes
Sue

KARNAC

First published in 2009 by
Karnac Books Ltd
118 Finchley Road, London NW3 5HT

British Library Cataloguing in Publication Data

A C.I.P. for this book is available from the British Library

ISBN: 978 1 85575 696 0

Edited, designed and produced by The Studio Publishing Services Ltd,
www.publishingservicesuk.co.uk
e-mail: studio@publishingservicesuk.co.uk

Printed in Great Britain

www.karnacbooks.com

CONTENTS

ACKNOWLEDGEMENTS

We would like to thank our professional colleagues and fellow members of the Advanced Organisational Consultation Society who, through word and deed, have contributed to our understanding of a mind-ful approach to consulting. In particular, we acknowledge the contribution of Knut Knutsen in helping to clarify our early thinking and the structure of this book.

As each of the chapters took shape, our contributors learnt about their consulting practice and were encouraged to engage with their own internal dialogue about what to report and what not. This is not easy, and we thank them all for staying with a sometimes challenging task. The extent to which we have been successful in gauging what is of interest is, of course, for our readers to judge.

Having access to an on-line repository for exchanging drafts and sharing thoughts and issues helped this process enormously, and we are grateful to Paul Owers for establishing and administering our Group Hub. The support of Phil Swann, Director of The Tavistock Institute until October 2008, is also acknowledged, as is the guidance, advice, and careful editing offered by our publishers, Karnac.

As an insight into consulting practice, this book would not have been possible without our clients. We thank them for working with and developing with us.

ABOUT THE EDITORS AND CONTRIBUTORS

Susan Rosina Whittle, BA, MSc, PhD, consults to individual managers, to project and work based teams, and to cross-boundary groups. She worked in inner city public and voluntary sector housing before moving into professional and organization development. For twenty years she has worked as an organization development consultant and participatory researcher in local government, manufacturing, health, construction, and the prison service. Her main interests are: sector level innovation; regulation and control; organization design; cross-boundary collaboration; individual, organizational, and inter-organizational learning; and the relationships between individual thinking and organization change. She is a member of the Core Faculty on Birmingham University's MSc in Leading Public Service Change and Organisational Development, and continues in her core faculty role with The Tavistock Institute's Advanced Organisational Change and Consulting Masters Programme. Email: sue@whittle1.karoo.co.uk

Karen Izod, MA, CQSW, utilizes multi-media approaches to her work with client systems, incorporating experiential inquiry and creative expression into her educational, consulting and coaching practice. Over the past twenty years, Karen has worked in sup-porting change within health and social care, local and national government, higher education, knowledge and media industries, and professional service firms. Her interests are located in the inter-faces between individual, organization, and society, in such themes as governance, diversity, and continuing careers. She is an organi-zational change consultant, KIzod Consulting, a member of the Core Faculty for the Tavistock Institute's Advanced Organisational Change and Consulting, and Co-Director for their Coaching for Leadership and Professional Development course. The early part of Karen's career was in social work and public sector management. She holds a qualification in Advanced Social Work from the Tavistock Clinic. Email: karenizod@lineone.net

Deborah Davidson works in the school of Social Policy at the University of Birmingham, where she is a Senior Fellow in Organ-isational Development and Leadership. Deborah's main interests are concerned with the management and organizational develop-ment of public services to realize citizen and service user outcomes, including black and ethnic minority communities. This also includes the development of people's leadership and authority in role, to lead and make changes in their organizational contexts at strategic, middle management, front-line, and community levels. Email: D.C.Davidson@bham.ac.uk

Kevin Dixon, BBA Hons, ACMA, MA, AOC. Kevin is Director and owner of Cross Boundary Solutions Ltd, Bournemouth. He has significant strategic change, programme, and project management experience gained in the public and not-for profit sectors in the UK and Ireland. Kevin's specialisms include accountancy, corporate governance, ethical business, strategy, and the behavioural aspects of individual, team, and organizational change. Kevin is currently working as education professional on a new international MBA programme at Bournemouth University. Additionally, he is a Trustee and Treasurer of the Environmental Law Foundation, and Treasurer and ex-officio Executive Committee Member of the Tavistock Institute's Advanced Organisational Consultation Society. Kevin is passionate about using human creativity and innovation to use technologies to create better working environments and ways of living. Email: kevinrdixon@btinternet.com http://crossboundary solutions.org

Veronika Grueneisen, PhD, is a psychoanalyst, training analyst DPG, IPA, organizational consultant, AOCS, partner (TELOS), and Chairperson of PCCA (Partners in Confronting Collective Atrocities). She works as a psychoanalyst, training analyst, and supervisor in private practice as well as teaching candidates in their psychoanalytic training. She has more than two decades of experience in adult education, with a focus on training for, and consulting to, middle managers in their leadership role. She has consulted to small and large systems, especially organizations in transition, mainly around conflict management and organizational development. Email: VeGrue@t-online.de

Ian Holder is a Director of 3C Partners and Non-Executive Director of a mental health organization. He is an organizational consultant, life coach, and counsellor, and also a Chartered Accountant with twenty years experience working as a director of multi-national companies. Over the past ten years he has worked with individuals and teams to manage change and develop their personal and business skills. Email: Ian@3CPartners.com

Nancy D. Johnson has over thirty years of experience in the fields of clinical, educational, and organizational consulting. She is a Licensed Professional Counsellor with a Master of Science degree in Psychology. As a founding partner of Crossroads Behavioural Health Associates, Nancy has also taught graduate courses at Southern Connecticut State University and provided Executive Coaching in such corporations as The Hartford Financial Services, Thomson Reuters, Thomson Healthcare, American Express, and Malcolm Pirnie Inc. Email: ndjcrossroads@yahoo.com

Libby Kinneen is Director of Organisation Development HSE West, Ireland. As an internal consultant, she enables professional groups to make transitions in response to sweeping organizational change. In addition, she has an independent consultancy practice focusing on role consultation and professional leadership issues.

Maria J. Nardone, President and Founder of M Nardone Company, is a licensed psychologist and Associate Clinical Professor at the State University of New York Downstate Medical School. She practises in New York City as a psychologist, psychoanalyst, and organizational consultant. She earned a BSc Mathematics with Honors in Psychology from Bucknell University and PhD in Psychology from Fordham University, completing post-graduate certification in psychotherapy and psychoanalysis at the William A. White Institute. She is a graduate of the AOC Programme, Tavistock Institute, London. Email: maria@mnardone.com

Paul Owers is an organizational consultant and founder of Catalysis Associates. He has fourteen years of experience working with senior teams, change leaders, groups, and individuals involved in complex, messy, often transitional states, supporting the organization to make sense of, and work through, challenging strategic and organizational change. His consulting focuses on turbulent environmental and organizational conditions and their impact on individuals, groups, and divisions within them. He has a particular focus on governance, strategic management, and collaboration across boundaries in order to maintain high performance. Paul holds an MA in Advanced Organizational Change and Consulting from The Tavistock Institute, and an MBA from INSEAD, Fontainebleau, France. He is a member of OPUS, an associate of Eden & McCallum in London, and of The Tavistock Institute, where he is also Deputy Chair of its Board of Studies. Email: paul.owers@mac.com

Jørn Hakon Riise has his own consultancy firm, is a Doctor of Business Administration (DBA), and specializes in organizational learning and organizational identity, including measuring, analysing, and developing organizational identities and cultures. He also works as a senior consultant in Assessit AS, which has its head office in Oslo and offices in other Scandinavian cities. He teaches marketing channels management and research methodology at The Norwegian School of Management, Oslo. He has consulted to clients in several sectors, including oil and energy, manufacturing companies, police services, national insurance, and more widely in programmes and workshops related to strategic HR issues. He has now a long-term assignment as an HR Manager for hire in a young company with a new and innovative product aiming for the global market. Email: jhr@unikogettertraktet.no www.unikogetter traktet.no

Antonio Sama is Visiting Fellow, Department of Social Work, Community and Mental Health at Christchurch Canterbury University, and Associate Professor at the University of Calabria. His consultancy interests relate to supporting and evaluating European funded initiatives in social care and regeneration. He is an active member of OPUS and runs their Calabrian based Listening Post.

Karol Szlichcinski is a management and organizational consultant and Director of K. Szlichcinski Associates Ltd. He has twenty years' experience of helping large and small businesses to clarify their strategy, plan their marketing, implement IT systems, and manage change. As well as being a member of the AOC Society, he is a Fellow of the Institute of Management Consultants, a Chartered Psychologist, and Chartered Marketer. He has served on the Board of Studies of the Tavistock Institute's Masters Programme in Advanced Organisational Consultation KS Associates, and as European Editor of the journal *Behaviour and Information Technology*. Email: karol@ksassociates.co.uk

Anjet van Linge is organization consultant and owner of Bureau Zee. Bringing over sixteen years' experience with international manufacturing, commercial, and service organizations, Anjet consults to projects such as the performance improvement of a call centre, the development of a culture of accountability in a refinery, or an energy company's journey to becoming a leader in sustainable energy. Her work sits on the intersection between leadership and organization development, and she invites leaders to explore the spirit and purpose that fuel the primary task of their organizations. She particularly enjoys working with global–local, centre–periphery tensions in complex organizations. Anjet holds an MA in Chinese Studies and an MA in Advanced Organisational Consultation from The Tavistock Institute/City University. Anjet is an associate of The Tavistock Institute. Email: anjetvanlinge@bureauzee.nl

Lawrence A. Vitulano is an executive coach and clinical psychologist with over twenty-five years of experience in a variety of fields relating to the growth and development of individuals seeking personal and professional advancement. He is an associate clinical professor of psychology at the Yale School of Medicine, and the former chief psychologist of the State of Connecticut Department of Children and Families, and president of the Connecticut Behavior Therapy Association. He serves on the Boards of several organizations, including the American Psychological Association, Southwest Community Health Center in Bridgeport, Connecticut, and the Bridgeport Council of Churches. Email: Lawrence.Vitulano@yale.edu

Maura Walsh is an organization consultant and executive coach with over twenty years' experience in organization and professional development. Her early career in learning and development focused on individual learning and professional development in the public, private, community, and higher education sectors. Since then, she has consulted to, and coached clients in, a range of organizations in the health, housing, built environment, manufacturing, pharmaceutical, and zoological sectors. Her main interests are in helping clients to make sense of complex scenarios and work effectively within and across boundaries, and in developing effective partnerships and collaborations within and across organizations. She is currently researching a PhD in inter-organizational collaboration in the Department of Management in Strathclyde Business School. She holds an MA in Education and an MA in Advanced Organisational Change and Consulting from the Tavistock Institute, of which she is an associate. Email: maura367@btinternet.com.

FOREWORD

Eliat Aram

This book is a collection of chapters written by experienced and thoughtful organization consultants, alumni of the Tavistock Institute's renowned AOC programme.

When I was invited to write the foreword for this book, as the new Tavistock Institute's Director, the title of the book, *Mind-ful Consulting*, grabbed my thoughts. What is "Mind" in this context, and what would it mean to be a "mind-ful consultant"?

Helped by the work of the social philosopher and American pragmatist, G. H. Mead, the "mind" is generally understood today as "the individual importation of the social process" (Mead, 1934). The individual's internal conversation of gestures, which Mead called the "I–me dialectic", is not possible by the individual alone, but is a part of the ongoing social process.

Bowlby, in his studies of the attachment patterns of children, used the concept of "mindfulness" to describe the healthy attention that a parent offers to a child. Mindfulness there refers to the capacity to hold an Other in mind and be open and receptive to their needs, nuances of changed behaviours, verbal, and sometimes nonverbal, communications.

Mindfulness is, therefore, inevitably a social and relational process. The authors of this book describe this well as they explain what they mean by the notion of "mind-ful consulting"; the containing and "working through" of the dynamics that emerge in the consulting process, which can be difficult, unbearable, or simply out-of-awareness.

The authors apply participative inquiry and reflexive methodologies to reflect on a range of consulting experiences, which illuminate vividly and draw close attention to the high degree of care necessary for "mind-ful consulting". Some of the key ideas and values embedded in this notion, which run through this book, are:

● that a mind-ful consultant is someone who works to raise the clients' awareness by challenging empathically, changing sensitively, and containing difficult emotions as these arise in the process of change;
● that a mind-ful consulting process between consultant and client system is reciprocal, mutual, and conversational;
● that a mind-ful consultant steps skilfully into the unknown with the client, who is an expert on their own experience.
● that the context of the consulting relationship is significant in informing its evolution, transformation, and sustainability;
● that mind-ful consultants are themselves engaged in an ongoing learning process;
● that mind-ful consulting is creative consulting and includes working visually and with other art forms to enrich the consulting process and its potential for transformational change.

Eric Miller, one of the founders of the programme in Advanced Organisational Change and Consulting (AOC), was my second supervisor for my PhD, in one of his many roles. After I was awarded my PhD, I went to visit him in order to give him a signed copy, as a token of my appreciation of his contribution to what I saw as an accomplishment. His response was that he was not interested in the doctorate thesis. "When you publish it as a book available to the broader community of practitioners," he said, "then I *would* like a copy."

Knowing how highly he thought of the published word and of organizational practitioners' capacities to reflect on their experiences, to make sense of their practice, and to make their words publically available, I know he would have been immensely proud of this edited book, which does exactly this.

I believe that *Mind-ful Consulting* is an essential read for any consultant who cares about the development of their praxis, and it is a refreshing asset to the scholarly writings within the Tavistock Institute's traditions.

Eliat Aram
Director, the Tavistock Institute of Human Relations
January 2009

The challenge of a mind-ful approach to organizational consulting

Sue Whittle

> "Granted that there are genuine emergent processes . . ., then we must accept real limitations upon what we can predict and also accept that we have to live for some time with the future before we know it"
>
> (Trist, 1997, p. 899)

This book illustrates how alumni of the Tavistock Institute's programme in Advanced Organizational Consultation (AOC) take up their professional roles in working with clients and with colleagues. Since 1993, the AOC programme has built upon the Tavistock Institute's traditions of (a) a psychoanalytically informed perspective on group and intergroup relations, (b) a model of organizations as socio-technical systems, and (c) an action research approach to inquiry, to support the development of consultancy competence for those working to change organizations. Over fifteen years, the design and content have changed as new perspectives have arisen.

In 2002, the programme was validated at Masters level through City University, London. This rekindled the theory/practice debate in the programme's educational design and in the assessment of competence to practice. It is in this context that the idea for the book emerged at an alumni event in Calabria, southern Italy, in 2005. The editorial steer was to make available to a wider readership stories about consulting "in an AOC way". Given the range of nationalities, base disciplines, sectors, market positions, product offerings, methodologies, and technical specialisms that comprise the AOC community, this was perhaps an impossible task. To that extent, this book is an intervention to codify our own practice.

In *Exploring Individual and Organizational Boundaries* (1979), editor Gordon Lawrence describes "The Tavistock Model" as a "heuristic framework for identifying and understanding what conscious and unconscious processes take place within and between groups of people" (p. 2). He goes on to say that while this representation is accurate, it is also misleading, in that the model is not static. To achieve a fuller picture, we need to look at how the framework is interpreted and embodied in the work of consultants. This has been our approach, not to retell the normative, but to invite phenomenological accounts of consultants at work.

Recent academic attacks on consulting as a world of impression management (Clark & Salaman, 1998) in search of certainty (Sturdy, 1997) that takes place in the liminal space of guru conferences (Bos & Heusinkveld, 2007; Czarniawska & Mazza, 2003), business dinners, and back-stage meetings (Collins, 2004) have done little to encourage consultants to speak about their challenges and difficulties. Books about success multiply, but books about problems and how to change consulting practice *in vivo* are rare (Gill & Whittle, 1993). The book aims to show how *mindful consulting* can support intervention and change that is developmental for both client and consultant. This approach, informed by both social and psychological aspects of organizational life, does not always lead to stories of resounding success. But, in moving away from the "grand narrative of progress" typical of many accounts of the work of consultants (Hassard, 1999), we aim to show how consulting practice informed by mindfulness—paying non-judgemental attention to tasks, roles, and boundaries, here and now—can help to achieve significant changes for clients and for consultants.

All authors are members of the AOC Society, and their associates. This alumni organization of the Tavistock Institute's AOC programme supports members' commitment to scholarly practice.

Meeting annually to peer review their consulting practice from their bases in UK, USA, Norway, Netherlands, Germany, Italy, and Ireland, they are in touch with current themes in consulting to organizational change in a multinational context.

This introduction presents a short exploration of the concept of mindfulness and describes how each chapter applies an understanding of a mind-ful consulting approach to supporting organizational change.

Exploring mindfulness

> When we are mindful, our attention is not entangled in the past or future, and we are not judging or rejecting what is occurring at the moment. We are present. This kind of attention generates energy, clear headedness, and joy. Fortunately, it is a skill that can be cultivated by anyone. [Germer, 2005, p. 5]

The idea of mindfulness, as a way of avoiding "mind-sets that unnecessarily limit us" (Langar, 1997), is finding resonance in a number of disciplines and professional practices: as an approach to learning (*ibid.*), a therapeutic technique (Hirst, 2003), and as a conceptual framework for shaping practice (Bentz & Shapiro, 1998; Shapiro, Carlson, Astin, & Freedman, 2006).

Its Buddist roots emphasize that "thoughts are just thoughts". Practising mindfulness can reduce the tendency to react unconsciously, or "mindlessly", and help to focus attention on experiences and events in the here and now, enabling individuals to be available for more intentional and conscious actions. (As described in the *Abhidhamma*, the Buddhist analysis of mind and mental processes, mindfulness has "the characteristic of not wobbling, i.e. not floating away from the object. Its function is absence of confusion or non-forgetfulness" (Bodhi, 2000, p. 86. See Wikipedia for a brief introduction.)

Langer describes how "Mindlessness sets in when we rely too rigidly on categories and distinctions created in the past" (1997, p. 11). This can result in "blindly going with the flow" (McLaren, 2004) and making sense of experiences through stereotyping and other debilitating, cognitive shorthands. These are significant issues for those involved in leading and supporting organizational change.

It is important to understand how mindfulness, as an approach to practice, differs from the idea of "mindset", essentially a cognitive device. Mintzberg (2004) has described an approach to professional management development using a framework of five mindsets: the reflective (about self); the worldly (about context); the analytical (about organization); the collaborative (about relationships); and the action mindset (about change). Working with mindsets in the plural can start to redress the reified mindlessness that sometimes infects management, and organization, development programmes. But prolonging the operating assumption that different mindsets (in Mintzerg's case, only five) are appropriate for different tasks, and can be put on like taking the right costume out of the wardrobe, seems to recreate those rigid categories to which Langer (1997) refers. Mindfulness is about putting together a wardrobe that has the requisite variety (Ashby, 1960) for the roles required of a consultant and then making sure that you do not just wear the items that are comfortable. It is also about not getting in stuck in narrow ranges of colours, textures, or styles, and acknowledging that taking risks with the wardrobe comes with the job.

It is on this last point that the difference between mindset and mindfulness is probably most apparent. The notion of mindset tends to be discussed primarily in terms of mental models (Eden, 1994; Senge, 1990), as cognitive devices relatively free of emotional and affective bonds (Dweck, 2007). As such, mindsets can be thought of as bundles of learnt responses more and less appropriate to specific contexts. They are archetypes (Greenwood & Hinings, 1993) or "world views", offering ready-formed routines of thinking and practice. It is this aspect that puts "mindset" most at odds with the idea of mindfulness.

> The disadvantage of a mind-set is that it can colour and control our perception to the extent that an experienced specialist may be among the last to see what is really happening when events take a new and unexpected turn. When faced with a major paradigm shift, analysts who know the most about a subject have the most to unlearn. [Heuer, 1999]

Germer (2005) describes mindfulness as "(1) awareness, (2) of present experience, (3) with acceptance" (p. 7). He offers the idea of *mindful moments* where

We can momentarily disengage from our activities by taking a long, conscious breath [and] . . . we can ask ourselves: "What am I feeling right now? What am I doing right now? What is most compelling to my awareness right now?" [*ibid.*, p. 8]

As such, mindfulness is "the opposite of being on autopilot . . . it is paying attention to what is salient in the present moment' (*ibid.*).

Weick and Putnam (2006) agree with Germer that mindfulness can be learnt, enabling practitioners to switch from operating on autopilot, in accordance with a well honed mindset, to becoming "more aware". Weick and Putnam's ideas were developed while working in high-risk contexts and with disaster scenarios, such as out of control forest fires. Putnam is concerned to understand why fire-fighters in high risk, stressful situations disregard obvious evidence from their experience and put themselves in danger:

Firefighters do not go to their deaths thinking in the morning that this is a good day to die, so let's violate the Fire Orders and other safety concerns . . . the real question is what were they paying attention to and basing their actions upon while embedded in a dynamic stressful situation? [Putnam, 2005, p. 2]

In their paper "On the benefits of being present", Brown and Ryan start with two assumptions:

(a) that individuals differ in their propensity or willingness to be aware and to sustain attention to what is occurring in the present and (b) that this mindful capacity varies within persons, because it can be sharpened or dulled by a variety of factors. [2003a, p. 822]

They suggest that "feelings of choice as well as feelings of enjoyment increase mindful attention to one's actions". Factors identified that dull mindfulness include "rumination, absorption in the past, fantasies and anxieties about the future" as well as doing multiple tasks, being preoccupied, and behaving compulsively or automatically.

A mind-ful approach to consulting practice has much in common with psychoanalytically informed approaches (Germer, 2005, p. 21). Both acknowledge the role of unconscious forces, emphasize the interplay between internal and external worlds, and hold the conviction that the route to change is via awareness and acceptance.

Brown and Ryan link mindfulness to a number of other constructs that have received attention in the world of consulting practice, such as emotional intelligence (awareness of and ability to manage one's emotions) and, from psychoanalysis, free association, "wherein attention 'evenly hovers' over the psychological landscape" (2003a, p. 823). They also distinguish mindfulness from reflexive thought, arguing that mindfulness is pre-reflexive and acting on the quality of consciousness, on "bare" thoughts and feelings, rather than within them. As such, mindfulness "is theorized to have little or no inherent relation to reflexive thought" (*ibid.*).

> The terms "unconscious" or "nonconscious" now appear with increasing frequency in mainstream journals. A picture has emerged of a set of pervasive, adaptive, sophisticated mental processes that occur largely out of view. [Wilson, 2002, p. 5]

Mindfulness also involves *remembering* but not dwelling in memories, or being stuck in the past. "This requires the *intention* to disentangle from our reverie and fully experience the moment" (Germer, 2005, p. 6). Being in touch with, and able to think about, our past experiences and relationships, while not being manipulated by them, resonates with the psychoanalytic concept of transference. Brown and Ryan describe this aspect of mindfulness thus:

> A key facet of the construct of mindfulness is the capacity for self-awareness; that is, highly mindful individuals are theorized to be more attentive to and aware of internal (psychological and physical) constructions, events, and processes than are less mindful individuals. Indeed, we and others have argued that effective self-regulation depends on this capacity for self-insight. [Brown & Ryan, 2003b, p. 833]

The capacity to identify and work with issues in the "here and now" that have arisen "there and then" is an essential competence for consulting to individual, group, and organizational change.

Mindfulness in consulting practice

A mind-ful approach to consulting practice is a way of avoiding both "mind-sets that unnecessarily limit us" (Langar, 1997) and the phenomenological pitfalls of "going with the flow". Non-judge-mental awareness of current sensory data, coupled with a relation-ship to the past and to others as further data about (issues in) the client system and our own professional practice, supports an exper-imental approach to sense-making (Weick, 2001) and to interven-tion design. "Reperceiving" (Shapiro, Carlson, Astin, & Freedman, 2006) is enabled both through the containment of premature thoughts and powerful emotions and the openness to novel (if sometimes uncomfortable) analyses afforded by a mind-ful approach (Bishop et al., 2004). In this way, the professional self is less motivated to protect itself and defend against negative judge-ments. This is not reflecting on practice, nor reflecting in practice (Schön, 1987). It is the temporary and orderly suspension of reflec-tion. Such a bounded engagement with clients and colleagues and our own experiences can support consultants' learning by doing and encourage a developmental approach to professional practice.

"Experience is not what happens to a man; it is what a man does with what happens to him" (Huxley, 1932). But consultants do not practise alone. At minimum, we are involved in dyadic relation-ships, as coaches and shadow consultants. More often, we work in and with small groups and sub-systems of larger organizations. Some consultants work corporately, with whole systems' change. So much (some would argue any) consulting practice is organiza-tional. Weick and Sutcliffe (2006) locate mindfulness as a property of organizations rather than individual psychologies. Their concept of "collective mindfulness" is understood as a way of organizing and has the following features:

- a preocupation with failure to guard against creeping compla-cency;
- a reluctance to simplify and become simple minded;
- a fostering of situational awareness and reporting of errors;
- a commitment to resilience, to resolve rather than be over-whelmed by errors;
- a deference to expertise rather than hierarchy, to expedite deci-sion taking.

Should these edicts be applied to consulting when practised in a mind-ful way? If so, what might this mean for engaging with and organizing the client and the client system in order to manage change? What implications are there for intervention design and the leadership and management of change processes? It is with these practical issues that the following ten chapters are concerned.

They describe the experiences of practising consultants as we struggle *against* going with the flow and work to be mind-ful in managing ourselves, in working with colleagues, and in working with clients.

Each narrative draws on thinking from the core disciplines of the Tavistock Institute's current AOC Programme: organization theory, consulting practice, and systems psychodynamics (Figure 1).

Consulting to large system change in the call centre of a utility company is the focus of Chapter One. Anjet van Linge's tale from the field describes how keeping in mind her clients' needs for containment and sense-making helped her intervene to bound the instabilities created by both planned and emergent change processes. She reflects on the challenges of a single practitioner con-

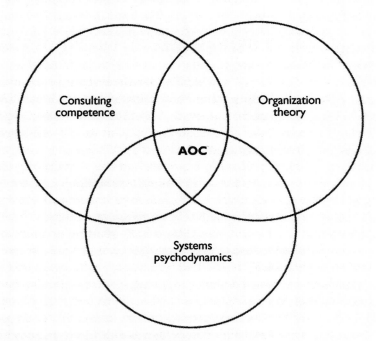

Figure 1. AOC programme core disciplines.

sulting to large system change and how being mind-ful of her own needs and behaviours offered insights into the needs of her client.

Jørn Hakon Riise reports on using identity auditing as a trigger for organization development and strategic change. Distinguishing between identity, image, reputation, and brand, Chapter Two describes how a gap analysis approach can help clients to be mind-ful of how identity, at both individual and organization levels, can shape planned and emergent changes. He identifies some of the difficulties in working with identity and offers recommendations to keep in mind.

In Chapter Three, Paul Owers writes about consulting to an organization in transition, in conditions of hyperturbulence. Using artefacts to articulate unspoken issues and assumptions, he describes how visual metaphors can be catalytic and containing for both consultant and client as they struggle to take up roles in complex and rapidly changing contexts. He demonstrates how consultants, in the way they work, can model several of the features of mind-ful organizations listed by Weick and Sutcliffe.

Using examples from their own experiences, Veronika Grueneisen and Karen Izod discuss the dynamics of hiring and being hired in Chapter Four. Through a series of vignettes, they offer examples of how mind-ful practice can be sharpened and dulled by a range of contractual circumstances and intrapsychic needs of both consultants and clients. "Reperceiving" the consultant–client relationship as a power-laden and dynamic dyad, rather than a service provider–consumer relationship, helps to bring the client out of the shadow of the consultant's narcissistic brilliance.

Karol Szlichcinski and Ian Holder adopt a life cycle perspective to describe their work, consulting to small business development, in Chapter Five. While using conventional management consultancy methods, they depict their approach as "being aware of and accepting the psychological experiences of the small business managers we work with and taking them into account in our consultancy". Being mindful of the individual and social psychologies shaping organizational life in small businesses informed their use of coaching, marketing, and IT based interventions to achieve individual, business, and sector level changes.

In exploring when consultants collaborate and when they do not, Maura Walsh and Sue Whittle turn their attention to the consultant system in Chapter Six. Often, this can fall out of consciousness, be taken for granted, and be subject to neither explicit scrutiny nor intervention. At worst, it can become undiscussable. Drawing on their own experiences, they offer a number of collaborative modes and propositions, and a model to help consultants become more mind-ful of the sorts of issues that may emerge when they are required to work together.

In Chapter Seven, Maria Nardone, Nancy Johnson, and Lawrence Vitulano write about their experiences of executive coaching as an organizational intervention. A long-term consulting relationship with their American based client has seen changes in the way external relationships are managed and internal power distributed, not only in the client organization but in the consultant system also. They argue that the benefits of team coaching arise from being mind-ful of the needs, individually and collectively, of coachees, coaches, and the organizational client. Managing the boundaries between these constituencies, and negotiating the inevitable issues that arise, is helped by the use of multi-disciplinary theories and models and maintaining a sharp awareness of the contracted task.

The distinction between mindset and mindfulness is illustrated in Chapter Eight. Through the perspectives of both consultant and client, Deborah Davidson and Libby Kinneen use the concepts of role mindset and political thinking strategies to describe what shaped their consultation and what helped the client to take up new roles in her organization in the context of turbulent structural and political change. Working with concepts from systems psychodynamics, organization theory, and social psychology, and keeping in mind organizational development needs, provided good enough containment to support exploration and change in health care services.

In Chapter Nine, Kevin Dixon states the case for ethical leadership in the accountancy profession. Adopting a whole-sector perspective, he offers a novel approach to professional development, using experiential methods and art. Mind-ful of the anxieties that need to be addressed by those working with "dirty" money, he describes his struggle to bring this approach to market in a sector heavily defended against change.

In Chapter Ten, Antonio Sama uses history, both as a source of data and a method of inquiry, when consulting to an Italian social enterprise that is stuck in its past. In a relationship of some ten years' standing, he describes how awareness of the need for a "painful break" to rework his own story in past roles with this client became a milestone in his development and a key element in consulting effectively to his client's need for change.

In the closing chapter, Karen Izod also engages with narrative as a paradigm for change and mind-ful consulting. She explores how consultants, coming with a sense of intention, can work to identify plots in their practice as a way of breaking from the autopilot of well rehearsed routines.

References

Ashby, W. R. (1960). *An Introduction to Cybernetics*. London: Chapman and Hall.

Bentz, V., & Shapiro, J. (1998). *Mindful Inquiry in Social Research*. Beverly Hills, CA: Sage.

Bishop, S. R., Lau, M., Shapiro, S., Carlson, L., Anderson, N. D., & Carmody, J. (2004). Mindfulness: a proposed operational definition. *Clinical Psychology: Science and Practice*, *11*(3): 230–242.

Bodhi, B. (Ed.) (2000). *A Comprehensive Manual of Abhidhamma*. Annotated translation of *Anuruddha* (ca. 1150). Onalaska, WA: Pariyatti.

Bos, R. ten, & Heusinkveld, S. (2007). The guru's gusto: management fashion, performance and taste. *Journal of Organizational Change Management*, *20*(3): 304–325.

Brown, K. W., & Ryan, R. M. (2003a). The benefits of being present: mindfulness and its role in psychological well-being. *Journal of Personality and Social Psychology*, *84*(4): 822–848.

Brown, K. W., & Ryan, R. M. (2003b). Why we don't need self-esteem: on fundamental needs, contingent love, and mindfulness. *Psychological Inquiry*, *14*(1): 27–82.

Clark, T., & Salaman, G. (1998). Creating the "right" impression: towards a dramaturgy of management consulting. *Services Industries Journal*, *18*(1): 18–38.

Collins, D. (2004). Who put the con in consultancy? Fads, recipes and "vodka margarine". *Human Relations, 57*(5): 553–572.

Czarniawska, B., & Mazza, C. (2003). Consulting as a liminal space. *Human Relations, 56*: 267–290.

Dweck, C. S. (2007). *Mindset: The Psychology of Success*. London: Ballantine.

Eden, C. (1994). Cognitive mapping and problem structuring for system dynamics model building. *System Dynamics Review*, 10(2–3): 257–276.

Germer, C. (2005). Mindfulness What Is It? What Does It Matter? In: C. K. Germer, R. D. Siegel, & P. R. Fulton (Eds.), *Mindfulness and Psychotherapy* (pp. 3–27). New York: Guilford.

Gill, J., & Whittle, S. (1993). Management by panacea: accounting for transience. *Journal of Management Studies*, 31(2): 281–295.

Greenwood, R., & Hinings, C. R. (1993). Understanding strategic change: the contribution of archetypes. *Academy of Management Journal*, 36(5): 1052–1081.

Hassard, J. (1999). Postmodernism, philosophy and management: concepts and controversies. *International Journal of Management Reviews*, 1(2): 171–195.

Heuer, R. J. (1999). *Psychology of Intelligence Analysis*. CSI Publications. Read online at https://www.cia.gov/library/center-for-the-study-of-intelligence/csi-publications/books-and-monographs/psychology-of-intelligence-analysis/art4.html

Hirst, I. S. (2003). Perspectives of mindfulness. *Journal of Psychiatric and Mental Health Nursing*, 10(3): 359–366.

Huxley, A. (1932). *Texts and Pretexts: An Anthology with Commentaries*. New York: Harper & Brothers. Downloaded on 8/1/2009 from *Encyclopaedia Britannica*, http://www.britannica.com/EBchecked/topic/277723/Aldous-Huxley/277723suppinfo/Supplemental-Information

Langer, E. (1997). *The Power of Mindful Learning*. Reading, MA: Addison-Wesley.

Lawrence, W. G. (Ed.) (1979). *Exploring Individual and Organizational Boundaries*. New York: Wiley [reprinted London: Karnac, 2002].

McLaren, C. N. (2004). Mindlessness in America: Ellen Langer and the social psychology of mindlessness. (Online), November 4, http://www.stayfreemagazine.org/archives/16/mindlessness.html.

Mintzberg, H. (2004). Third-generation management development. *TD*, March: 28–37.

Putnam, T. (2005). Deep psychology: the quiet way to wisdom. In: B. W. Butler, & M. E. Alexander (Eds.), *Eighth International Wildland Firefighter Safety Summit: Human Factors – 10 Years Later*. 26–28 April. Missoula, MT: The International Association of Wildland Fire, Hot Springs, SD. Download at: http://www.iawf

online.org/summit/2005%20Presentations/2005_pdf/Putnam. pdf

Schön, D. (1987). *Educating the Reflective Practitioner.* San Francisco, CA: Jossey-Bass.

Senge, P. M. (1990). *The Fifth Discipline: The Art and Practice of the Learning Organization.* New York: Doubleday, Currency series.

Shapiro, S. L., Carlson, L. E., Astin, J. A., & Freedman, B. (2006). Mechanisms of mindfulness. *Journal of Clinical Psychology, 62*(3): 373–386.

Sturdy, A. (1997). The dialectics of consultancy. *Critical Perspectives on Accounting, 8*: 511–535.

Trist, E. (1997). The next thirty years: concepts, methods and anticipations. *Human Relations, 50*: 885–935.

Weick, K. (2001). *Making Sense of the Organisation.* Oxford: Blackwell.

Weick, K. E., & Putnam, D. (2006). Organizing for mindfulness: Eastern wisdom and Western knowledge. *Journal of Management Inquiry, 15*(3): 275–287.

Weick, K. E., & Sutcliffe, K. M. (2006). Mindfulness and the quality of organizational attention, *Organisation Science, 17*(4): 514–524.

Wilson, T. D. (2002). *Strangers to Ourselves.* Cambridge, MA: Harvard University Press.

CHAPTER ONE

Making sense of instability: a case study of change in a large system[1]

Anjet van Linge

Introduction

T his chapter describes a case study of large system change in the call centre of a utility company, in which a combination of planned and emergent change resulted in substantial business improvement as well as a mix of anxiety and personal development for some of its leaders. The instability stirred up by the crisis and amplified by some interventions became a potential space for finding new ways of working. Looking at the process over two years, four significant themes emerge:

- the importance of bounded instability in creating potential space for developing new solutions to existing problems;
- the need for containment at various levels in the hierarchy;
- the importance of sense-making in bounding instability, and mobilizing the organization;
- the challenges and chances of working with a large system as a single consultant.

As the approach to the change process was largely emergent, I highlight the main characteristics of each phase and the interventions that unfolded before exploring these themes in the text.

Context

The organization is a utility company, operating in the period immediately after deregulation of its market. The call centre maintained the organization's direct contact with customers, supporting its retail and business-to-business divisions, and was being held accountable for the organization's poor reputation. It faced a backlog of tens of thousands of bills, and many customers were extremely unsatisfied. The company was under the scrutiny of the regulator, who had imposed a deadline for clearing the backlog. While competitors were in a similar position, this company attracted most attention and took most of the pressure in the national press, being called the "champion of chaos". At the start of year one, a new Call Centre Director had been appointed, the fifth in five years.

The story of the change process in three phases

Phase I: Changing expectations and amplifying instability (January–June, year one)

The situation at the beginning of this phase is summarized in Table 1.

During his first month, the new director tried to get an understanding of the backlog problems: ". . . the [staff] were promising the customer that somebody would address their problem and I just followed the trail—walking through the organization. And I'll be honest, I didn't have a clue. There were hundreds of really motivated people, trying to do their utmost, but they had no answers for these customers, and mostly when they picked up the phone, the customer only got angrier."

At the end of this month he asked me to process consult to his first Management Team (MT) off site. The MT had developed a

Table 1. Summary of the situation at the beginning of Phase I.

Business environment	Perceived problems	Interventions
• Turbulent through press focus on backlog of many thousands of bills • Company labelled "champion of chaos" • Ambition to be best in country not in line with reputation • Customer satisfaction very low	• Post deregulation systems very complex • It is not ok not to know the answer • Repeating pattern of short-term fixes • Management Team (MT) manage own backyard only—no felt joint accountability • Operational managers have more insight but appear held back by MT • Operational focus on efficiency, not on quality	• Operational focus on 1st time right • Two *MT Off Sites* to set direction and basic structure • Four *Management Days* to diagnose root causes, identify solutions by process chain and design basic structure of new organization • Design team of operational managers for *Management Days* • Allocation of operational managers to "process teams" across boundaries of existing departments

culture in which it was important to know the answers to any questions and to keep your territory clean, even when that did not contribute favourably to the overall result. This first off site was different. The agenda consisted of one question: where do we want to be in two years' time? Not used to exploring options, the MT members found it hard to use the space creatively, but did ultimately agree on the concept of an organization based on client processes. This idea was further developed in a second off site a month later.

At both off sites the director surprised the MT members by injecting changes towards the end of each event. At the first, he suggested that maybe an organization along process chains was achievable in six months rather than two years. The second time, he announced that he was going to ask the operational managers to get involved in the organizational design (Figure 1), a suggestion that also surprised me.

In individual interviews I realized that most MT-members experienced the meetings as both a creative and terrifying experience, but outside the meeting, found it hard to hold on to the common ground that had been created. The surprises destabilized the MT-members, and made them unsure about their roles in the process.

In the four subsequent Management Days, operational managers were asked to diagnose the root causes of the crisis, and to design the basic processes to address them. They worked in process teams chaired by MT members and formed on the basis of the basic design the MT had done during their off sites. This structural intervention eased MT anxiety somewhat and would later facilitate the transition to a new organization. None the less, sharing the organization design with the operational managers instead of being solely responsible for it as MT members left them feeling bypassed.

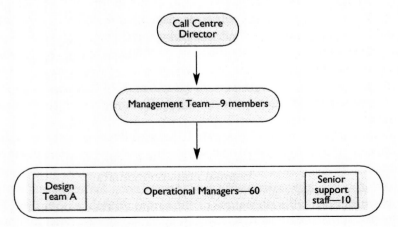

Figure 1.   Operational design, Phase I.

In the design of the Management Days they were bypassed as well, as ten operational managers (design team A) were invited by the director to take up his task. The director chaired the team and I process consulted to it, as well as contributing to the design of the four days. In practice, the operational managers in the design team were "really keen to be asked", and "very happy to contribute", but found it hard to take up a strong design role, trusting that "when you say this works, I am sure it will".

In the Management Days, a mix of large group intervention methods enabled the operational managers to think creatively, and, challenging together, to solve conflicts they used to refer to the MT in order to produce the basic design of a new organization. With design team members acting as facilitators during the Management Days, the MT members had no visible role, and seemed to act out their anxiety about this by dominating some of the plenary conversations. At the same time, the joint work between the operational managers generated enormous energy and "capacity we did not know we had". This co-operative attitude extended only occasionally beyond the Management Days. In an organization that traditionally had operated strongly hierarchically, such different ways of working appeared unsettling for MT and operational managers alike.

Like the MT members, I also struggled with my role. How much grip did I need on this process? Could I let the design team facilitate large group events? How could I enable this organization to learn to work with this seemingly unpredictable director, who was so radically changing the rules of the game?

Phase II: Containing anxiety and building skills (July–December, year one)

Table 2 summarizes the situation at the start of Phase II.

At the end of Phase I, the regulator's deadline to clear the bills' backlog was met. This created space to begin implementing the new process-based organization.

A root cause of the backlog had been a leadership style characterized by listening insufficiently to the needs of clients and the operational front line. Because a new organizational structure without a different style was unlikely to improve performance sustain-

Table 2. Summary of the situation at the beginning of Phase II.

Business environment	Perceived problems	Interventions
• Backlog crisis addressed but customer satisfaction still low • Benchmark data indicate cost pressure	• Leaders lacking ability to coach and listen to frontline needs • Need to implement new organization design in way that is congruent with participative design process • Need to tap potential of team leaders for continuous improvement	• Focus still on 1st time right, "no fixes" • Implementation of new organization • Three *Leadership Days* for skill development and sense-making, including peer coaching on implementation of new organization • Bi-monthly *MT Off Sites* to enable MTs to make sense of their role in the change process

ably, three Leadership Days were designed to help operational managers develop.

Together with a colleague, I tailored the three Leadership Days to the needs of the moment, mixing skill-building activities (how to ask better questions, surface assumptions, and understand own and others' mental models) with opportunities for making sense of the reorganization process, and practising skills to communicate to staff. No design team was involved this time.

While they had experienced different ways of working in Phase I, operational managers were unsettled by the explicit expectation to coach their teams, ask questions instead of telling teams what to do, and to involve team leaders in decision making about the implementation of the reorganization. The reorganization also stirred up anxiety.

The MT appeared in turmoil at the start of Phase II, and took no part in the design process, with the exception of the Communications Manager, a new MT member. The team seemed incapable of taking decisions without the director, and was confused about its own authority. Contained time to reflect on individuals' (emotional) journeys in previous months enhanced the MT members' ability to take up their leadership role again, which was reflected in their part-time facilitator role on the third Leadership Day.

My role changed in Phase II. Initially, I wondered why I had not noticed the MT members' very obvious need to work through their own anxiety and explore how to take up their leadership role in the face of changing expectations. Had my own role confusion stood in the way of this? Enabling a difficult conversation between the team and the director strengthened my credibility with the team. As facilitator of the Leadership Days, I now had to shift between process consultant and facilitator. I kept wondering how I could enable the MT to be visible as leaders, and yet leave space for the operational managers to develop the coaching focus expected of them.

Phase III: Emerging patterns and coalitions (January–December, year two)

The situation at this point is summarized in Table 3.

At the end of Phase II, the organization had implemented a new process-based organization and significantly increased its customer satisfaction ratings. The MT started to lead differently, while the operational managers were still struggling. The core of the desired change, responding to client needs by listening and leading differently, had barely reached the 230 team leaders (Figure 2).

Having reflected on using and bypassing hierarchy in Phases I and II, I suggested a process for the design and delivery of the team leader programme that consciously used both.

The director asked a design team of team leaders (design team B) what they "needed to do their job as best they could". Like the operational managers in design team A in year one, the team leaders in design team B responded cagily at first, asking permission to talk and speaking about "the needs of the organization" instead of their own. Seeing a chance to further develop what they had learnt in Phase II, eight operational managers and the Communications

Table 3.

Business environment	Perceived problems	Interventions
• Customer satisfaction ratings increase • Benchmark data indicate high cost of service	• Results of new processes in some chains but limited bottom up initiation of improvements • Operational managers struggling to develop as coaches of team leaders • Team leaders unclear about reason for new organization and their changed role in it • Performance improvement sustainable?	• Team Leader Development Programme of three modules to include: facilitator training; basic design by facilitators; final design by facilitators, design team, and MT reps • Design team of team leaders set specification • Operational Managers form facilitator team • Establish rhythm of MT days throughout year

Manager volunteered as facilitators. The MT authorized them to work with design team B's specification.

The design days were core to Phase III. They started with facilitator training (led by my colleague and me), followed by a process in which design and facilitation teams together with an MT member tailored the building blocks of our basic design to meet their needs. The process required co-operation across hierarchical levels. This brought to the surface expectations of, and assumptions about, each other's roles. This was such a confronting and rewarding experience that the teams sought to recreate it for their colleagues. As the year progressed we increasingly took a process consulting role in the design process, with the design of the final module being guided only by some design criteria. Throughout the

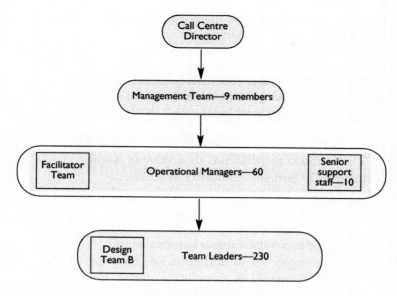

Figure 2. Structure of operational design at the end of Phase II.

modules my colleague and I coached the facilitators, helping them to make sense of their experience.

Team leaders were enthusiastic about the programme, feeling supported in taking up their changing role. At the end of the year about 70% of the team leaders' direct reports identified a different way of leading, though they were not prepared to say that this was due to the programme. The organization achieved the highest customer satisfaction ratings in the sector, and the changes were the start of a process of ongoing improvement.

My role during this phase shifted again from leadership expert to process consultant. In the second half of the year the facilitation team was my main interface with the organization, though I maintained contact with the director. My main concern was to ensure that facilitators did not learn at the expense of team leaders, and to find a way to enable learning to spread beyond the core group.

Three critical aspects of managing large system change

The data offered is only a fragment of the richness of a two-year consulting project. None the less, three themes stand out for me as aspects that are important in managing large system change processes.

On bounded instability as potential space

In his work about complex responsive processes, Stacey (1992, 2001) illustrates the difference between the control necessary for day-to-day operations and the bounded instability required to enable strategic change. Bounded instability, the border area between equilibrium and out of control disequilibrium, is the space in which new patterns of behaviour can emerge, new coalitions can form, and change can take shape.

The backlog of many thousands of outstanding bills created some sense of instability, further enhanced by the threat of a regulator deadline. Yet the new director did not assume he needed more stability, but rather created further instability. The rationale was to unfreeze the system, not so that *he* could change it, but in order for it to change itself. In addition to the crisis, instability was actively created by changing the rules of the game called leadership (listen, ask, coach, instead of tell and answer), through bypassing levels in the hierarchy and devolving organizational design to operational managers, and by creating space at management and leadership days for new patterns of interaction and behaviour to emerge. Especially at the start of the process, instability was also amplified by repeated surprises, such as suggesting that a new organization was possible in six months instead of two years.

Bringing together people from across departmental silos and levels in the hierarchy to work together created a new, unstable space *in between* the pressing problem (the backlog) and the solution (something different, though no one knew yet what). This in between space was not unlike that which Winnicott calls potential space (Davis & Wallbridge, 1991).

Phase I, management day 1. The director made a video about a disabled, unemployed customer who had been handled extremely badly. After showing it, he said: "I will not work for an organization that does this to customers. I will not take responsibility for an operation that has this many chances to correct the mistake and apologize, and still screws up. . . . And I don't know the answer. So, I'll ask you in teams to think this through, and tell me in four weeks what we need to do to prevent this from ever happening again, and do things right the first time". The video shocked the room into a few minutes silence.

This statement legitimized not knowing and opened up the organization's potential space. In the space created by the instability and the legitimacy of not knowing, "playing" (Davis & Wallbridge, 1991; Winnicott, 1958) became possible, leading to new interactions across old silo boundaries, and creative new ways to design client-facing processes.

Stacey says that instability must be bounded for it to remain creative and not degenerate into explosive chaos (Stacey, 1992, 2001). Bounding factors were the continuation of operational MT meetings, the rhythm of the management and leadership days throughout all three phases, the contained setting of these days themselves, and the structure of the process teams that later formed the basis for the new organization, as well as the fact that these teams were led by MT members. Within these boundaries instability can lead to growth. In the bounded instability new coalitions can form and become powerful.

> *Towards the end of Phase III.* Faced with business pressures, the MT contemplated cancelling the last leadership day for some team leaders. Members of the design team and facilitators felt cancelling would be contrary to anything the programme in Phase III had represented. The informal leader of the design team led a successful confrontation with the MT and the director, in which she spoke passionately and authentically, feeling backed up by her colleagues in the design team and the facilitators. Her visible personal growth throughout the year, combined with the way she was able to voice the concerns of the design and facilitation team, convinced the MT to continue as planned.

On levels of containment

Winnicott (Davis & Wallbridge, 1991) says that the limitations of playing are determined by the players' capacity to contain the experience of play. This seems to have been the case in the call centre. Bounded instability and organizational change brought inevitable difficult emotions, anxieties, and contradictory feelings. Containment is the provision of a holding environment in which these can be experienced and explored creatively without becoming destructive, and without giving in to the desire to fix or dismiss them (Bion, 1985; French & Vince, 1999).

Like the boundaries around instability, clear structures, clarity about task, role and organizational hierarchy can act as containing factors (Obholzer, 1999). As such, containment is a core task of managers and change agents, requiring the non-anxious presence of those doing the holding (Neumann, 1999).

The director was explicit about his own need for containment.

After Phase III, interview with Director. "I've learnt how it takes a lot for me not to project who I am, or what I need into a situation, but to really try to understand what the other person's position is and what they need. And I've found that the most difficult, because I was often confronted with my own unrest, the pressure and my own judgements I make as a person—which is not always productive. So that is my leadership challenge."

However, he did not make his processing explicit. His presence appeared at times so non-anxious it seemed to deny others' rights to their anxiety.

Possibly as a result of this, I did not create explicit opportunities for contained working through of the anxieties the instability generated in MT members. Yet the regression in the MT's behaviour at the beginning of Phase II signified that perhaps, for them, living in the instability had become nearly unbearable.

Phases I and II. During Phase I, the design team was drawn from operational managers "to create some upward pressure". The MT members felt they were responsible, but had no control over the design or outcome of the process. They acted out their anxiety by speaking a lot at the first three management days. In one design team meeting, the director said his "patience was running out with this old behaviour". The MT members felt they were losing authority and at the start of Phase II the team was in turmoil. It was incapable of taking decisions during the director's holiday, and sometimes seemed unable to speak when he was in the room. At a reflective Off Site, I consulted to a difficult discussion in which they explored their anxieties about the emergent nature of the process, their fear of losing control in contrast to the excitement of new possibilities, and their confusion about their role. They also touched on the difficulty they had in relating to a director for whom this all seemed so easy.

Attending to their need for containment did not take their feelings away, but shifted their ability to take up their leadership roles throughout the rest of Phases II and III.

Another container can be hierarchy. Hierarchical structure and distribution of power provide a boundary around the self-organizing process (Stacey, 1992), and are crucial for good organizational functioning (Jaques, 2006). However, creating instability by bypassing the hierarchy makes it lose its containing function. This was visible during Phases I and II. In Phase III, I paid more attention to what I have started to call levels of containment.

Figure 3 describes how the instability was created through asking the design team for a design specification (1), which was offered to and authorized by the MT (2), who also authorized the facilitation team (3). Instability was recreated by leaving the design mainly to the design team and the facilitator team (4), which took its role seriously and not only facilitated the team leader modules (5) but also organized an operational management day (6) on its own initiative.

In addition MT off sites and facilitator training provided space for exploring the contradictory emotions of leading without controlling (MT members) and facilitating "your own" team leaders (operational managers) (Figure 3).

Using the levels in the hierarchy in this way meant they did not constrain instability, but became levels of containment that contributed to making the instability bearable and creative. If containment is not attended to and levels of containment are not appropriately used, the organization seeks other ways to contain its anxiety, by acting out, falling back on old routines, or other defensive mechanisms that may stifle creativity. This works in two directions.

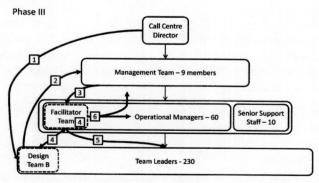

Figure 3. Levels of containment in Phase III.

Phase III. Inspired by their own learning, the facilitators initiated an additional leadership day for operational managers. Taking their autonomy seriously, the facilitators had agreed only the objectives with the director and taken charge of the design themselves, with my process consultation. The day included a dialogue with team leaders about what support they needed. At some point one operational manager asked a question the director felt reflected old behaviour. Not trusting the facilitator to further enquire, and to handle the situation with his colleagues, the director immediately intervened forcefully, silencing further discussion. Later, he suggested that being aware of how the facilitators wanted to lead the process and what my role would have been in containing it if it had gone off the rails might have helped him not to step in.

Upon reflection, it seems that the upward pressure from facilitators had further amplified instability. Not contracting clearly with the director meant he lost his ability to contain his anxiety and behaved defensively.

On the role of sense-making

Sense-making helps people to turn their experiences into something intelligible, and reduces ambiguity. It is like cartography, taking the elements in the landscape and turning them into a map to guide your movements. It is characterized by high visibility, high choice, and irreversibility (Weick, 2001).

Phase II, day two. In day two, the managers were asked to use an iceberg technique to move from seeing events, patterns, and structures to understanding underlying mental models. In teams, they had difficult discussions about how their way of thinking influenced their behaviours. They then collated their insights on to one large iceberg and collectively realized why they often did not work together (no confrontations, own yard clean, I know better, I have to know the answer, etc.), and came to see that they needed fundamentally to shift their way of thinking in order for the new structure to work.

This day in particular helped people to understand and commit to the rationale behind the new organization, which provided some containment for the anxiety generated by the new expectations of them as leaders.

Sense-making *between* people with various roles and levels in particular can mobilize the organization.

Phase III. The facilitator team had spent a day exploring how to facilitate discussions about different styles of leadership. In their struggle to differentiate between the styles, they were confronted with their own mental models about them. The following day they were joined by members of the design team and the MT. Together they designed role plays to illustrate the different styles. This led to vigorous discussions that created insight into their mutual roles, and helped them understand how these related in the service of the organization's task: "We are all just people, we just have different roles". This experience became the basis for the design of module three.

In this example, the confusion between the roles was addressed, albeit within the confines of the small group that contributed to the design. In the evaluation at the end of Phase III it became clear that where team leaders, operational manager, and MT member in one department had contributed to the design days, their joint sense-making had significantly affected the success of the change process.

In the facilitator team, the shared experience of tough training and module facilitation had taught facilitators "to trust the group", and "experiencing that makes us lead differently". The opportunities to make sense of these experiences created a powerful sub-culture in the team. It started to act both as an attractor (new volunteers joined the team) and as a source of envy. Its influence in the system was significant, and its upward pressure for a more facilitative style of leadership stirred up new instability.

Sense-making thus contributed to the organization's ability to contain itself, and amplified some of the patterns that could emerge in the potential space of bounded instability.

Reflections on the role of the consultant

My role as consultant changed continuously throughout the process. In Phase I, I was, like the MT, concerned about my grip on the process, and I was often surprised by the actions of the director. While I had contact with various sub-systems (MT, design team and the large group), as single consultant it was hard to make sense of all the signs other than through the director's lens. Not having contracted explicitly enough with him about my role at the start of the process might have led me to get "too far in" the system and contributed to my feeling insufficiently contained to provide the containment the MT needed.

The MT in turmoil at the start of Phase II shocked me back into my consulting role on the boundary of the system. Attending to the MT's need for containment enhanced my credibility, and enabled me to take up both a process consultant and a leadership expert role, as long as I differentiated clearly between them.

My colleague, who joined the work in Phase II, was an ex-business manager who had been trained as a facilitator of skill-building sessions. She saw me as the lead consultant. While our collaboration offered some space for sense-making between us, I needed to contain her anxiety more than we were able to offer mutual containment. I still felt as if I were a single consultant in a large system. Perhaps, in my "singularity", I mirrored the individual position the director had found himself in, receiving minimum containment from his superiors and experiencing envy from his peers.

In Phase III, I paid more attention to the balance between instability and boundaries, and to the levels of containment outlined above. In this phase the facilitator team became the axis of transformation in the organization. The training, supervision, and process consulting I did with them became symbolic for the new way of leading the organization was seeking: at a distance, enabling, coaching, and intervening only when the learning of one group (facilitators) was at the expense of the other (team leaders), or when unconscious undercurrents obstructed the work. The anxieties I felt when the facilitator team delivered their first module mirrored how they felt about taking a different leadership role, and this became a useful source of information.

Looking back, it seems that the magnitude of the task, combined with my singularity in the system, overwhelmed me initially. Feeling that I was a single consultant, however, also necessitated the use of design teams and facilitation teams, both for doing the work and as a micro-cosmos of sense-making. This, I believe, became a strong factor in the success of the change process.

Final thoughts

This chapter offers four main areas of attention when managing large system change.

1. Bounded instability can create potential space in which an organization can change itself. Finding the right balance between interventions that amplify instability and those that provide boundaries is, therefore, critical.
2. Containment can bound the instability and is crucial for enabling an organization to use it creatively. In addition to specific time and space for contained working through of difficult emotions, levels in the hierarchy can serve as levels of containment, contributing to the creative use of the unstable space.
3. Sense-making can enhance an organization's ability to contain itself and allow new patterns of behaviour and coalitions of leaders to emerge. Creating opportunities for sense-making between levels in the hierarchy, in particular, can mobilize the organization.
4. Even as an individual consultant in a large system, one's own thoughts and feelings, one's losing and refinding of role and task, are an indication of the needs of the system, and need to be attended to in order for the change process to be effective. In order for this source to be accessible, the single consultant needs to attend to her own needs for containment.

Note

1. This chapter is a registered activity as part of "Refreshing the Tavistock Institute's Intellectual Traditions".

References

Bion, W. R. (1985). Container and contained. In: A. D. Colman & M. H. Geller (Eds.), *Group Relations Reader 2.* Jupiter: A. K. Rice Institute.

Davis, M., & Wallbridge, D. (1991). *Boundary and Space, An Introduction to the Work of D. W. Winnicott.* London: Karnac.

French, R., & Vince, R. (Eds.) (1999). *Group Relations, Management and Organization.* Oxford: Oxford University Press.

Jaques, E. (2006). *Requisite Organization, A Total System for Effective Managerial Organization and Managerial Leadership for the 21st Century.* Baltimore, : Cason Hall.

Neumann, J. (1999). Systems psychodynamics in the service of political organizational change. In: R. French & R. Vince (Eds.), *Group Relations, Management and Organization*. Oxford: Oxford University Press.

Obholzer, A. (1999). Managing the unconscious at work. In: R. French & R. Vince (Eds.), *Group Relations, Management and Organization*. Oxford: Oxford University Press.

Stacey, R. (1992). *Managing the Unknowable: Strategic Boundaries Between Order and Chaos in Organizations*. San Francisco, CA: Jossey-Bass

Stacey, R. (2001). *Complex Responsive Processes in Organizations, Learning and Knowledge Creation*. London: Routledge.

Weick, K. E. (2001). *Making Sense of the Organization*. Malden, NJ: Blackwell.

Winnicott, D. W. (1958). *Through Paediatrics to Psychoanalysis*. London: Karnac.

CHAPTER TWO

Organizational identity, identification, and learning: how can organizations take advantage of the dynamic relationship between them?

Jørn Hakon Riise

Introduction

Organizational learning and organizational identity are related and interdependent, both as concepts and as organizational activities or properties. That identity construction is a function of learning and development activities applies to both individuals and organizations (Riise, 2006). The life of individuals and organizations can be perceived as a continuous dynamic process within which a struggle between learning and identity is taking place. Identity represents continuity or stability, while learning represents change or instability. Organizations seem torn between a need for consistency of perspective and behaviour, and a need for flexibility and capacity for change (Stacey, 1996). Organizational learning and organizational identity are relevant and useful concepts to explore the dilemma organizations experience between a need for change and a need for continuity over time. Learning, as a concept, captures the essence of an organization's need for change, while the concept of identity captures an organization's need for stability.

If engaged in the challenges created by their environments, individuals and organizations have to face dilemmas related to their identity. Learning—at least of a profound kind—implies a change of identity as well. In a world that continuously changes, individuals and organizations will face the dilemma of what part of their identity to stick to and what part to change. They might be partly unaware of these changes taking place, because individuals and organizations to a large extent, more or less consciously, adapt to their environments, willingly or unwillingly.

An unawareness of such identity changes going on might in the long term lead to individuals and organizations lacking a clear perception and understanding of themselves and their own responses and reactions to their environments. A lack of consciousness of themselves and their priorities will, as a next step, make it difficult to relate to and address their environments in an appropriate way. Just as individuals need some stable perceptions of themselves, so do organizations. Perceptions are socially constructed, meaning that perceptions are developed by, and built on, a basis of continuous feedback from environments. In terms of change, the processes of learning, identity strengthening, or any kind of identity change are all nourished by feedback from the environment. A deliberate process of identity clarification and of identity strengthening must therefore take into account and include activities of searching for feedback. Feedback will often imply that gaps between how individuals and organizations perceive themselves and how others perceive them are uncovered. Such gaps can then be used actively to trigger and initiate learning.

So far, I have related the concepts of identity and learning to both individuals and organizations. The rest of this chapter will deal with identity and learning related only to organizations, even if I think the same perspectives apply to individuals. My research and consulting practice focuses on organizational identity and organizational learning.

Organizational learning, change, and identity

A type of learning is referred to as problem-solving learning—"learning to learn". This kind of organizational learning requires collective reflection on governing rules and assumptions. According to Bateson (1972), learning of this type involves attainment of knowledge about the development and the meaning of habits and is rarely possible for individuals because it occurs only in religious and spiritual experiences or in psychotherapy. This kind of learning normally demands stimuli from others; organizations can offer arenas or settings for this kind of learning to take place.

The need for change is frequently imposed on organizations from the environment and is often met by resistance from organizational members. Reger and colleagues (1994) ask why dedicated members resist beneficial change, and their explanation is that mental barriers hinder fundamental change. Change is interpreted through mental models, and a particularly powerful mental model is the set of beliefs members hold about the organization's identity.

> Identity beliefs are critical to consider when implementing fundamental change because organizational identity is what individuals believe is central, distinctive, and enduring about their organizations. These beliefs are especially resistant to change because they are embedded within members' most basic assumptions about the organization's character. [Reger, Mullane, Gustafson, & DeMarie, 1994, p. 34]

Reger and colleagues link different change modes to change of identity (*ibid.*). According to them, past prescriptions give managers two approaches to implementing change: incremental or revolutionary, neither of which provides satisfactory results for most firms in dynamic environments. They think a third option is needed, and they call this proactive, mid-range approach the *tectonic* implementation mode. Table 1 shows the environmental conditions in which each implementation mode is most effective. Reger and colleagues argue that mid-range processes are the most appropriate for most firms in today's dynamic environments.

In light of the shortcomings of incremental processes, many CEOs opt for a revolutionary approach to change. However, these kinds of change processes rarely achieve planned results because they challenge employees' basic assumptions about the very nature of the firm. They require a blank page approach to change, but companies are not blank pages. Change programmes that threaten core beliefs about the organization will be met with resistance,

Table 1.   Comparison of different change modes.

Environmental conditions	Change process	Change magnitude	Change objective (organizational identity)
Stable	Incremental	Minor fine-tuning or adjustment	No change or piecemeal changes in organizational identity
Turbulent	Tectonic	Moderate	Significant changes, building on existing elements of organizational identity
Crisis	Revolutionary	Massive	Complete replacement of organizational identity

unless the organization is confronted with an overwhelming crisis. The perplexing question is why dedicated members resist beneficial change. Resistance can be understood by examining the role of mental models in general, and then by exploring the concept of organizational identity and its relationship to the implementation process (*ibid.*).

Why organizational identity is desirable

Research and organizational practice relating to organizational identity and organizational identification has a fairly short history, but it has clearly increased in the last 10–15 years.

I have done some research myself on organizational identity (Riise, 2006) as well as applying this approach and related concepts in my consultancy practice. Knowledge and experiences acquired from my practice and from my research supports the idea of organizational identity becoming increasingly relevant for organizations struggling to improve their functioning in various ways.

A major reason for this increasing importance of, and interest in, organizational identity is the growing competitive environment surrounding organizations. In an increasingly competitive market, organizations and their products need to stand out in order to be noticed. To be singled out from its competitors, an organization needs to develop its distinctness; it needs to focus on and to develop its uniqueness. To develop an organization's uniqueness implies analysing and developing its identity.

There is also a growing interest, awareness, and level of expectation concerning how organizations handle their physical and social environments. Organizations are expected to take more care and to behave according to the norms and values of their stakeholders and society as a whole. It is expected that organizations show integrity; that there is some degree of congruency between what they say and what they do, and between their internal and external practices.

First, I present various elements of the organizational identity concept in order to show its multi-faceted capability of capturing a broad range of organizational issues. As a start, it is useful to explain two main constructs of interest, one being organizational identity and the other organizational identification.

Organizational identity and organizational identification

An organization has to put effort into developing its identity in order to make its uniqueness more explicit and clear to stakeholders and to be perceived as reliable. To become attractive in the long term presupposes that an organization makes clear what it stands for. First, the core or the soul of the organization has to be made clear to its employees and potential employees. What has become more evident recently is that organizations have to compete more strongly for the competence they need. This means that an organization has to become attractive, not only to its customers or end-users, but to the kind of candidates it is searching for to become its employees. This is a market of its own kind, and in this market a strong and clear organizational identity is a competitive advantage.

An organization's identity is characterized by Albert & Whetten (1985) as "a self reflective question" (who are we anyway, as an organization?). Identity captures the essential features of an organization. They concluded:

those features could be summarized in three major dimensions: Organizational identity is (a) what is taken by organizational members to be central to the organization; (b) what makes the organization distinctive from other organizations (at least in the eyes of the beholding members); and (c) what is perceived by members to be an enduring or continuing feature linking the present organization with the past (and presumably the future). [Gioia, 1998, p. 21]

According to this definition, one important dimension of organizational identity is its durability or continuity.

In addition, customers' degree of satisfaction depends on the quality and the characteristics of an organization's products and services, and on the extent to which they live up to their expectations.

Organizational identification can be defined as "a cognitive link between the definition of the organization and the definition of self" (Dutton, Dukerich, & Harquail, 1994, p. 242). Another way of defining organizational identification is that "organizational identification occurs when an individual's beliefs about his or her organization become self-referential or self-defining. That is, organizational identification occurs when one comes to integrate beliefs about one's organization into one's identity" (Pratt, 1998, p. 172). Pratt proposed that two conditions are necessary for organizational identification to occur: "(a) the individual must perceive the organizational identity to be salient, and (b) the individual must self-categorize him or herself in terms of his or her organizational identity" (ibid., p. 194).

Organizational identification is often confused with other concepts, one of them being organizational commitment. The concept of organizational commitment can be used to differentiate the concept of organizational identification. The reason for using organizational commitment as a comparison for the concept of organizational identification is that organizational commitment seems to be used more often than similar concepts to describe individuals' emotional attraction to, and involvement in, organizations. Organizational commitment can be defined as "a psychological bond that a member forms with his or her employing organization that is characterised by behavioural, emotional, and cognitive consistency on the part of the member" (ibid., p. 176).

How is organizational identification differentiated from organizational commitment? The main difference, as defined by Pratt (1998), is that *organizational identification is organization-specific*. Identification explains the individual–organization relationship in terms of an individual's self-concept; organizational commitment does not. The two concepts trigger two very different questions. Organizational commitment is often associated with "How happy or satisfied am I with my organization?" Organizational identification triggers the question "How do I perceive myself in relation to my organization?"

Organizational identification deals more with the inner core of individuals than organizational commitment. While organizational commitment is equated with the "acceptance" of organizational values and beliefs, organizational identification is equated with "sharing" or "possessing" organizational values and beliefs. Organizational identification presupposes that individuals have values and beliefs of their own that are of importance to them. Individuals with strong values and beliefs therefore cannot easily just accept organizational values and beliefs that are not congruent with their own. Rather, they will search for organizations that share their values and beliefs. If they succeed in this, they can identify with the chosen organization; they can see something of themselves in the organization.

In order to initiate and nourish individuals' identification with an organization, an organization will have to clarify and strengthen its identity. It is difficult to identify strongly with an organization if its identity is weak, unclear, or hidden. So, organizations should strive to clarify and strengthen their identity in order to attract both customers and employees. But, maybe even more important, a strong and clear identity is necessary in order to trigger and exploit the latent energy of their employees.

An organization's identity needs to be challenged and changed

An organization's identity represents to some extent the continuity of that organization. However, a strong identity is not developed without struggle and resistance. Just like immunity to diseases, the building of a strong identity—be it individual or organizational—is often a result of resistance and effort that have challenged the identity. An organization's identity is socially constructed. This means that, just like individuals, an organization cannot develop a perception of itself, of its identity, without feedback and correction from its environment. An organization has to make choices in terms of what should be its primary activities, values, beliefs, competences, image, and positioning. But, at the same time, the organization cannot function well without understanding and relating in a good manner to its stakeholders and other environments.

How an organization can clarify and strengthen its identity

Several studies have shown that many managers are very frightened or anxious about having the reputation of their organization or of themselves damaged. But what can a manager and the manager's organization do in order to prevent its reputation from being harmed or to improve it? One way is to let knowledge about the organization's reputation be confronted with the organization's identity. Research and experience have shown that the awareness of gaps between an organization's identity and its reputation, or between its identity and its image, can trigger organizational learning and change if this awareness is developed and applied by the organization.

Figure 1 shows how an organization's identity influences, and is influenced by, its related organizational properties of image, reputation, and brand. Organizations will normally experience that gaps will be developed between these attributes. The question is to what extent, and how does the organization handle these gaps?

Consulting to organizational identity

Studies seem to indicate that CEOs and other managers are strongly preoccupied with their organization's reputation or image, and that they fear to have their reputation damaged. They seem to be more sensitive to how they are perceived by others than to how they perceive themselves. In order to succeed, most organizations, of

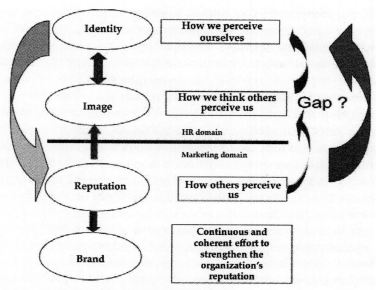

Figure 1. Using identity gaps as learning triggers.

course, depend on how they are perceived by various stakeholders. But there is a link between how organizations are perceived by others and how they perceive themselves. How they perceive themselves, their identity, is the source of their preferences, priorities, and behaviour, and therefore it will in the long run have an influence on their reputation.

Even so, the fact that their organization's identity is important to their reputation does not seem to bother managers. There are several reasons for this lack of awareness and attention among managers. One is that people in general seem to be more susceptible to others' perception of them than their own perception. But, when dealing with organizations, a more serious and professional attitude and practice concerning identity development could be expected. Organizations should have access to professional expertise on how to analyse and develop their organizational identity. This could be in the form of internal personnel employed by the organization, or it could be in the form of services delivered by external consultants.

Unfortunately, this is often not the case. Most organizations do not seem to have access to this kind of expertise, and they do not give this issue high enough priority. It could have been the responsibility of the HR function to work with an organization's identity, but in most cases they do not seem to have this expertise, and they do not apply the kind of comprehensive approach needed for this purpose. As a comparison, many organizations have access to professional expertise to assist them in their external affairs. For quite some time marketing has been a well-known area of expertise, and organizations normally give this function high priority. While marketing activities and reputation building are often promoted by the marketing department of an organization, there is a lack of specific professional expertise with the capacity required to initiate and promote activities intended to build an organization's identity.

From my years of experience working within the HR field, a lack of professional approach with respect to an organization's identity is a serious deficiency for any organization, and this deficiency also undermines the legitimacy of the HR function. So, because I perceive organizational identity as a basic issue for any organization to address, develop, and strengthen, and because addressing identity enables an organization to clarify its priorities and direction to stakeholders internally as well as externally, I have chosen to work with organizational identity as a consultant.

Two approaches

Various approaches to data gathering are available when working with an organization's identity. Both qualitative and quantitative approaches, or a combination of the two, are applicable.

Ideally, a qualitative approach would be preferred in order to capture the diversity and complexity that characterizes an organization's identity. Just like individual human beings, organizations are unique entities because of their complexity. People have to find their unique way through their life based on the challenges and the tasks they face and how they handle them. How these challenges are handled is a determining factor in the development of a person's identity. The same applies to an organization. Clarification and strengthening of an organization's identity implies a learning process, preferably a deliberate learning process.

A qualitative approach would imply interviews with a sample of managers and employees of an organization. They would then be invited to describe their perceptions and experiences of the practices of the organization. However, normally organizations are not willing to invest the time and money necessary to collect this kind of data and, in my experience, managers are generally more sceptical about the credibility of such data. Quantitative data are more likely to be accepted by CEOs and other managers, and are often more easily integrated in existing reporting systems than qualitative data.

About 130 organizations in Norway have so far applied the identity index and similar tools. Many of these organizations have reported positive results. Their experiences indicate the usefulness of measuring, analysing, clarifying, and strengthening their identity to achieve better results. However, in this chapter I prefer to present examples from organizations that have had some difficulties in trying to apply the approaches and tools described here. It is useful to learn from mistakes.

The quantitative approach

When a quantitative approach to an assessment of an organization's identity strength is chosen, an index or a measuring instrument consisting of six statements or items is applied. These six statements relate to the organization's purpose or primary activities, its vision, values, position, core competence, and image. Members of an organization show their degree of identification with the organization, scoring on a scale of 1–5. The results of their scores represent the identity strength of the organization. These results are fed back to the organizational members for interpretation and design of measures for organizational improvement.

Successful application of such an identity index depends on the organization's willingness and ability to explore the data openly with the aim of finding the best measures of improvement. In my experience, this represents a significant challenge for many organizations. When using ordinary employee surveys, organizations and their managers show signs of fear for having to deal with these results, and when a measurement of the degree of identification with the organization is applied, the results seems to scare managers even more. One reason for this reaction might be that the identity index is a short and simple instrument that quite clearly shows the conditions of the organization with respect to its identity strength. The identity strength is central to an organization's long-term success. This instrument can easily be used to compare the results of one organizational unit with the results of any other. It can also be used to compare the extent to which an organizational unit, or the organization as a whole, makes progress over time, or to compare with other organizations.

The simplicity of the measuring instrument in terms of how results are presented makes differences explicit and comparisons easy. This can be frightening, especially for managers who are held accountable for the results of their units. I experienced an example of this fear when doing an assessment in a large public sector organization in Norway. This assessment included measurement of the identity strength of the organization, a measurement of engagement, and of knowledge sharing. These are all measured by the use of similar indexes, each of them containing six statements or items and a scale covering a range from one to five.

The results were to be presented at a meeting for the top management and for managers from all over the country. The presentation included a comparison of the results between the various units and district offices. The top management was quite resistant to revealing the results showing the comparison between units and districts. They feared that the managers would not be prepared. The matter was discussed several times, and the conclusion from these discussions changed each time. Just before the results were to be presented, the decision was made that the results showing the comparisons between the units should be on the screen for a very short time, therefore not giving the people present any chance to study them or to discuss the results.

This organization has just measured the identity strength for the second time, and they are now analysing the results to see if they have had any improvements. This is the right way to work. The measurement of the identity strength should be done regularly. It normally takes 3–4 measurements in order to reach a good level for the identity strength if the organization works seriously. Some organizations measure their identity strength annually, while others do it quarterly. I would recommend that organizations do it quarterly, because these measures can be applied as early warning indicators of conditions developing in the wrong direction.

A quantitative approach was also applied in an organization of a very different kind. This was an organization that runs several large and different franchise chains selling fast food, newspapers, and periodicals. The franchisees were perceived as customers by the organization. I was invited to design and execute a survey that included a measurement of the strength of the organization's identity, engagement, knowledge sharing, and reputation. Identity, engagement, and knowledge sharing is measured internally, while the organization's reputation is measured externally among the franchisees.

To benefit from the data gathering and feedback intervention, these measures need to be handled according to designed procedures and followed up using a specified process. Management as well as employees are trained in how these tools work, how they should be interpreted, and how measures of improvement should be developed. In this specific organization, the management did not follow the procedures. They chose to apply this tool in a way that undermined or strongly reduced the possible effects of the intervention. It seemed as if the management was not at all interested in learning about internal measures of identity and using them to improve the organization. They seemed to be much more interested in using the results for strategic purposes relating to the organization's reputation among the franchisees.

For this organization, a relevant question to ask is if there is a sufficient willingness to learn. An organization is supposed to be willing to explore the results of the measurement in order for these tools to have an effect. This organization has decided to measure the identity strength quarterly. It is still in an early stage of obtaining the procedures of this approach, and it remains to be seen if they will succeed in taking advantage of applying it.

The qualitative approach

An assessment of the strength of an organization's identity and of the organizational members' identification with the organization could also be made by the use of a qualitative approach. This approach uses in-depth interviews in which the respondent is invited to present information and perceptions in line with his or her preferences. An organization's identity is usually quite mixed and complex. The organizational members represent some of this complexity, with a wide range of experiences and perceptions. They are the carriers of the identity of the organization. A qualitative approach is more sensitive to this complexity.

I have applied this approach in an organization that functions as a competence centre, working with children and adolescents with learning disabilities resulting from various types of brain injuries. The organization had about forty employees, most of them educated as teachers and psychologists. This competence centre had, like similar centres all over the country, previously been merged as a result of political decisions made by the government. When I worked for the organization, almost ten years had already passed since this merger was imposed upon them. The majority of the members of the organization still shared a perception of being divided into two groups. This perception was not due to, or aligned with, the formal structure of the organization; it was based on differences in terms of identification. Since the organization was the result of a merger between two organizations, members of the organization still identified with the organization they came from originally. A new and common organizational identity had not developed.

I conducted open interviews with eighteen of the forty employees, and this division in terms of a different identification was very visible. This experience shows that, in mergers or in other types of structural change, the concepts of identity and identification are of specific importance and useful tools for understanding what is going on.

The merged organization also faced other challenges as a result of political decisions imposed on them. It had been decided that the professional role of the employees should change. They should no longer work with the children and adolescents directly; they should rather work as coaches or consultants to the teachers and counsellors who were working with the children and the adolescents. This change was perceived by the employees as a threat to their professional identity. Their professional identity seemed to be very much based on the contact they had with the children and adolescents, and on the experiences and the direct feedback they received through this way of working. A loss of this direct contact with their clients was seen as if they were losing part of their souls. Their professional identity had for a large part been built on seeing that their professional assistance was needed, and that it made a difference to the clients' situation. After the change in policy and guidelines relating to how they were supposed to work, they could no longer observe directly the effects of their work.

In addition to employees, a sample of customers of the competence centre was interviewed, and the data collected from them were compared with the data collected from the employees. This was done in order to identify any gap between the organization's identity and its reputation. If any gap were identified, it was supposed to be used as a stimulus to improve and strengthen the identity of the organization. This organization was, however, burdened and distressed by the organizational members being very occupied by the divisions in the members' identification and by the changes in the professional role of the employees that had been imposed on them. As a result, members were not very responsive to the feedback from their environment. When members of an organization become confused about both their organization's identity and their own professional identity in this way, they tend to lose focus on, and become disconnected from, the primary task of the organization.

But despite these strong barriers to change, I was, five years later, informed by the managing director that the organization had improved and that the process of working with the organization's identity had been helpful.

This example brings the focus back to the main purpose for applying the concepts of organizational identity and organizational identification; the clarity and the strength of an organization's identity is critical for the organization's ability to deal with its primary task and to reach its goals.

Conclusions

Both results from research studies and experiences from my consulting practice indicate that organizations that work deliberately to clarify and strengthen their identity experience effects in the form of improvements. These activities might be triggered by some kind of crisis, but, as shown in Figure 1, a crisis is not an ideal way of triggering change.

It is much better for an organization to work continuously and deliberately to let their identity be challenged, clarified, and strengthened. A challenge to an organization's identity does not normally happen by itself; it needs a trigger. Tools for measuring the strength of identity and identification could function as such a trigger.

My experience as a consultant working with the analysis and building of organizational identity is that organizations that actively apply these measuring tools frequently and, according to the procedures specified (reporting of results, spending time in interpreting them, and identifying measures to be implemented), do report performance improvements. But there still are very few organizations working this way in the sense of trying to clarify their identity, in the sense of deliberately searching for data about their identity strength, member identification, and reputation, and in the sense of applying such data as triggers for development.

I shall sum up my experiences from working as a consultant assessing, analysing, and strengthening the identity of organizations and with employees' identification with the organization in the form of some recommendations.

1. In order to fulfil their primary tasks, organizations need to learn and change.
2. Organizational learning and change of a profound kind implies that the organization's identity is being challenged and changed.
3. The most important task for any organization is to work continuously to clarify and strengthen its identity.
4. Working to clarify and strengthen their identity is crucial to organization development, and the concept of organizational identity is a useful tool to stimulate change and to work with in order to improve their results.
5. Organizations need to apply well-designed methodologies and tools to trigger and encourage learning and change.
6. Working with organizational identity should have both an internal as well as an external facet.
7. There is, or should be, a dynamic relationship between the internal and the external perception of the organization. The internal

perception is represented by the organization's identity and the external perception by the organization's reputation. An awareness of a gap between the two can be used as a trigger for addressing this dynamic.

8. There is often a resistance among members of an organization against having their organization's identity challenged and changed.

9. If the management fear that the results of the assessment of the organizational identity might uncover results they will not like, they are inclined to deliberately or unconsciously use the tools for purposes other than for improving the organization.

10. This is why it is of great importance that an organization acts according to the procedures and guidelines of this approach.

References

Albert, S., & Whetten, D. A. (1985). Organizational identity. *Research in Organizational Behavior, 7*: 263–295.

Bateson, G. (1972). *Steps to an Ecology of Mind—A Revolutionary Approach to Man's Understanding of Himself.* New York: Ballantine Books, 1992.

Dutton, J. E., Dukerich, J. M., & Harquail, C. V. (1994). Organizational images and member identification. *Administrative Science Quarterly, 39*: 239–263.

Gioia, D. A. (1998). From individual to organizational identity. In: D. A. Whetten & P. C. Godfrey (Eds.), *Identity in Organizations—Building Theory through Conversations* (pp. 17–32). Thousand Oaks, CA: Sage.

Pratt, M. (1998). To be or not to be: central questions in organizational identification. In: D. A. Whetten & P. C. Godfrey (Eds.), *Identity in Organizations—Building Theory through Conversations* (pp. 171–208). Thousand Oaks, CA: Sage.

Reger, R. K., Mullane, J. V., Gustafson, L. T., & DeMarie, S. M. (1994). Creating earthquakes to change organizational mindsets. *Academy of Management Executive, 8*(4): 31–46.

Riise, Jørn H. (2006). An examination of the relationship between organisational learning and organisational identity. Thesis submitted as part of the degree of Doctor of Business Administration (DBA), Henley Management College/Brunel University.

Stacey, R. D. (1996). *Strategic Management & Organisational Dynamics.* London: Pitman.

CHAPTER THREE

Consulting in hyperturbulent conditions to organizations in transition[1]

Paul Owers

Introduction

This chapter explores the concept of organizational turbulence in conditions of rapid change. Reviewing theory on "hyperturbulent" environments, it looks at the relentless effects that turbulence has on organization and its concurrent affect on system psychodynamics. It considers passive responses to these conditions as well as adaptive strategies.

It draws on recent consulting experience in the communication industries and discuses managing "self" as instrument in the face of potentially overwhelming issues in large systems.

The use of visual metaphors to abstract and represent "system-in-the-mind" is presented as a useful means of processing and relating to the high volume of information required to surface and work through issues of interdependency in consulting to strategic change in hyperturbulent conditions.

It argues that visualization can be catalytic and containing, aiding the reconceptualization of complex, messy, and transitional states of organization for both consultant and client. The use of visualization as a support tool to enable transformational change is considered.

A personal experience of entering an organization in turbulent conditions

"We just go with the flow around here"

These eight words began to inform my understanding of an organization in hyperturbulence. I could sense the "flow". The organization seemed unanchored, and I mirrored that feeling, in danger of drifting in the current. It was difficult to have a grounded conversation anywhere in the organization. The flow was strong, shifting, and difficult to describe other than as a swirl of interconnected and interdependent issues related to the strategic debate about the future of the organization.

The organization was a large technology company (CommCo) with several thousand employees across Europe. Changes in market structure and opportunity were forcing a review of the structure of the company, with large divestment opportunities driving a change in revenue streams and business model. As a result, the client was changing its European management structure and clarifying organizational design and accountabilities.

The organization was energized to change but the energy was in flow around the system and not yet engaged in the work or grounded in shared understanding.

What might be underneath the phrase "We just go with the flow around here", a collective statement of behaviour relating to the status quo? What might be interpreted from these few words?

"We" I interpreted to indicate a collective, cultural phenomenon, adopted, often unconsciously, as the "way we do things in this organization". It denies or excludes "I", and suggests the collusion of self with the situation and the system. Individual responsibility for letting "the flow" continue was lost. The collective dynamic appeared to be acting as an organizational defence against the uncertainty and complexity.

"Just go with"—I interpreted this as "don't try to resist the flow. It is too strong". This experience presented a dilemma. In organization consultancy, part of the role of the consultant is to focus awareness on difficult or counterproductive organizational dynamics, bringing the dynamics into collective awareness, where they may be worked through to effect change. In order to understand the dynamic, I needed to go with or into it, to "go with the flow" and learn more. The dilemma was the risk of being engulfed by it; unable to hold my role sufficiently to catalyse the organizational work required. If I was unable to keep sufficient external objectivity, to see and otherwise sense the organizational issues present in the situation, it would be difficult to bring an external perspective, which was what I was contracted to do.

"Around here"—I interpreted to mean not "here" (where I am but "all around where we are"). This led to a sense of a collective among or in the middle of the "swirl", feeling powerless in the face of the difficulties.

I reflected on what the "flow" was. What was in it? What was its nature? What kind of dynamic was it?

Task and team

Contracting with CommCo to agree scope, objectives, and deliverables was challenging. It was difficult to gain an unequivocal view of the issues to be addressed. The issues differed depending on the individual executive. Linked to this it was difficult to see who the embodiment of my "client" was. This alerted me to a systemic issue of accountabilities in relation to this change.

There were multiple layers to the contracting process. My client was a senior executive in temporary charge of the change programme pending the planned senior management reorganization. An external interim manager had been appointed to build and develop the change programme. My contracted task was to design and develop the transitional organization to lead and support governance of the strategic change, allocate accountabilities, and develop a framework for decision making across Europe.

CommCo had difficulty shaping, staffing, and forming this key change project. At the individual level, potential staff members felt the project was too risky to join. It took two months to agree the staff for a first phase of the work. HR staff dealt with high levels of detailed queries about roles' duration and tackled reasons why members could not join the team. (This same phenomenon occurred between the first and second phases, where first phase staff returned to their country roles and many did not come back. A temporary project office built for eighty people became a group of seven people while the organization tried to regain commitment to staffing a second phase. There were difficult feelings of endings and voids, abandonment, or lack of care by the organization.)

The objective was to build a central project team tasked with developing a multi-country cross-functional agenda spanning all aspects of the change process. This perspective was difficult for any one country to develop alone. To support the process, I conceptualized the central change team as a referent organization (Trist, 1983), aware of the potential political difficulties relating to existing authority structures that this could present (Sydow & Windeler, 1998). With representation from the countries, the team could develop the integrated picture of meta-issues in the change that were common but affected each country differently. My objective was to achieve a more cohesive approach to the changes. However, the role of the central change team and its relationship to the countries and their authority structures required further development.

The central project team could be conceptualized as a microcosm of the wider organization (Alderfer, 1982). It comprised fifty-five people representing all functions and territories. It was rich ground for observation of organizational dynamics and for the interpretation and development of working hypotheses about what was happening, why, and what interventions might support progress.

I took up a role to work on the contracted task at the same time as observing the difficulties and dynamics within the central change team as they conducted their tasks on behalf of the system as a whole. This dual role as participant–observer enabled me to observe the group and organizational dynamics first-hand in the here-and-now. What I observed illustrated the underlying organizational issues that needed to be addressed in the transitional organization form.

Conceptualizing the client system

Accountabilities in relation to this multi-country change appeared loosely defined in the wider organization; perhaps an organizational defence (Menzies Lyth, 1988), a collective strategy of coping with high levels of uncertainty, complexity, and inter-dependency. It may have provided greater organizational flexibility, but this also gave leeway to "the flow".

In these early stages, I did not sense "leadership" in the context of managing functioning boundaries around groups that could contain issues; to regulate what, how, when to work on which issues and why. Concurrently, and interlinked, I did not sense sufficient followership, functionally engaged on the priorities and direction agreed with "leadership". Interfaces between groups were also under-developed and representation at those interfaces unclear, further complicating work on issues across group boundaries. I did not perceive an adequate level of differentiation of the constituent parts of a new or transitional organization that my emerging hypothesis suggested needed to emerge out of the old status quo. It was as if the organization needed to catch up in its sense-making of the situation.

I noticed that dialogue in the central change team and in the wider organization seemed superficial. When involved in discussion, I sensed members of CommCo were not talking authentically about the "real" or deeper issues. I could intuit many unspoken questions. Necessary levels of dialogue seemed lacking. When I touched on my hypothesis of the work to be done, often across organizational interfaces, there was a sense of avoidance. It was as if, just below the surface of awareness, but well within recall, was an individual and collective understanding of "the work that is being avoided". I hypothesized that this work needed clarification, greater containment, and clearer accountabilities and responsibilities in order to support the development of leadership on these tasks.

Linked to the sense of individual withdrawal from dialogue about the issues, groups were withdrawn, too. As work in the initial stages progressed, frustrations emerged between groups in the large project team meetings. These were expressed as unmet needs from other groups. Elements of these needs seemed unrecognized by the other groups, leading to a sense of disconnection between them. In the open-plan office I observed team interactions. I was struck by how few cross-functional team meetings occurred outside of the large team meetings. The functional groups seemed insular and dialogue between them negligible on a day-to-day basis.

There was a sense that the central change team knew that large system change management techniques, such as issue tracking, would be largely ineffective, but that a project plan was still needed, perhaps as a transitional object. The high degree of inter-dependency implied that something more fluid was needed, a more comprehensive inter-group, and inter-country dialogue with collective sense-making occurring in parallel.

Touching the organization in this way, at this time, gave an impression of its "texture" (Emery & Trist, 1965; McCann & Selsky, 1997): politically sensitive and fragile, interdependent but loosely linked, withdrawn from one another. The system and its groups seemed under-contained, with the energy in the system and the issues turbulent, swirling, and ungrounded.

What is turbulence and why is it difficult to consult to?

In a non-turbulent (or placid) environment, uncertainty is manageable in day-to-day operations and organizations have sufficient adaptive capacity to overcome changes in the environment. However, as uncertainties increase, a turbulent environment emerges and continuing organizational adaptation may become problematic (Emery & Trist, 1965). Turbulence has an impact on the organization in its entirety, within and between divisions or departments, the groups or teams that comprise them, and individuals within them.

Differences in adaptive capacity may emerge between component parts and changes in one part of the system can create new pressures on other interlinked parts. Turbulence is, therefore, diffused in its sources and effects. Additionally, this turbulent state is not a threshold state passed through by all organizational units in the same way or at the same time. The more interdependence between component parts, the more serious the implications for doing work and managing change.

This is an unevenly experienced condition, difficult to predict and manage. In my experience it has been possible to observe a "vortex", a turbulence moving around a system, engaging and overloading different groups at different organizational interfaces at different times. At times it has seemed possible to have a sense of where it will appear and where it will go next. It is this relative adaptive capacity, and the fact that members and groups pass through their threshold of capacity at different times, in different ways, that sets off internal organizational turbulence and associated systems psychodynamics.

This unpredictability makes turbulence difficult to consult to at the component part or group level. Taking a system-as-a-whole perspective raises the analysis above the level of individual component parts. It raises awareness of "other" in the system. It helps to keep interdependency in the mind along with challenges others are facing.

As turbulence increases further, a hyper-turbulent environment emerges (McCann & Selsky, 1997). Hyper-turbulence can threaten to overload organizational sense-making capacity, sparking difficult organizational dynamics as a "fear of not-knowing" pervades the system. These difficult system psychodynamics can threaten the capacity of an organization to adapt even further.

Hyper-turbulence has been described as the dynamics that emerge, not from the interactions of component parts, but from the social field itself (*ibid.*). An analogy is the response of the Millennium Bridge over the River Thames in London, which developed an unforeseen dynamic property, a wobble, in relation to the mass of the general public walking across it for the first time. This is not a property of the people walking across the bridge, but a formerly hidden property of the bridge in relation to "people". Applying this analogy in organizational terms, hyper-turbulence may be experienced as a feeling of being unanchored, of issues being "not grounded" or ungroundable.

The challenge for the consultant is to be sufficiently grounded to work without collusion and to remain sufficiently contained to go with the flow, to observe and analyse the flow, but not be subsumed by it.

Sense-making

In my experience with organizations in such conditions, the turbulence happening outside appears to be mirrored inside the organization. These two dynamics become interlinked. The external environment was in a state of rapid flux and turbulence. New technologies and competitor advances caused step changes, and the resulting turbulence in the market challenged strategy setting, direction, and leadership.

Weick (2001) argues that the environment and the organization can be viewed as one "universe". There is a continuum between what is "outside" and what is "inside", and these dual layers of analysis are inseparable. If the field is turbulent, and organizational members are an integral part of that field, the divisions and groups within which members organize are also liable to experience the effects of turbulence and the interrelated affects of systems psychodynamics.

As I worked with CommCo and reflected on my experience, I noticed similarities to turbulent and hyper-turbulent organizational states described by McCann and Selsky (1997), Baburoglu (1988), and Angyal (1941). Angyal's systems model describes three dimensions of organization along which maladaptive responses to turbulence can occur: vertical, progression, and transverse.

The vertical dimension relates to "surface *vs.* depth; what is apparent *vs.* what is underneath the surface, perhaps hidden or unspoken. At one extreme, dialogue, actions, and interactions are superficial, without much substance or engagement at any depth with the issues at hand. At the other extreme, dialogue is deep and meaningful, open and non-defensive, fluid and creative in its approaches to new information and the development of shared understanding. This resonated with my experience of the shallow depth of dialogue I heard in CommCo. A sense that the questions are known but unspoken, perhaps avoided, was hanging in the ether waiting for a questioner to speak them. Refocusing the organization on these questions was key.

"Progression" is the "means–end" dimension. In this dimension the maladaptive response results in an activity being aborted before completion. Means–ends become loosely coupled, if at all. This had startling parallels to difficulties in staffing the project. It also grounded my experience of the project team dispersing at the end of a first phase and the organization struggling to re-form it for a contiguous phase two. The dissipation seemed to be a visible phenomenon of some disruption or discontinuity in the organization's ability to hold together the means–end dimension. The unresolved political debate about the future direction of the company, and the resulting ambiguity and ambivalence may have stimulated this particular maladaptive response.

"Transverse" is the lateral dimension. It defines the positioning of the parts and their relatedness. With large-scale change, critical interdependencies between organizational parts come sharply into focus. It is critical for the lateral dimension to function as well as possible. In times of turbulence, component parts of the system seek to reduce complexity by limiting the challenges and difficulties they receive in relating to interdependent parts. It was striking how diffuse group boundaries became in CommCo, and how ambiguous representation within them increased. I observed the avoidance of accountability and the taking-up of multiple accountabilities across group boundaries, blurring them and confusing representation at group interfaces. Clarifying representation and accountabilities is a critical step in the consulting process.

Here, then, is a concept of disturbances, or maladaptive responses to turbulence, in three dimensions of an organization as a living "whole", of an organizational system facing a new demand, close to overload, with stresses and strains between and within parts linked to differences in adaptive capacity. These difficulties can evoke passive behaviours of withdrawal, dissociation, and superficiality, suggesting a need to stimulate adaptive activity in the form of deeper dialogue, engagement, collaboration, and greater integration.

The difficulty with collaboration is that it creates further demands on cognition. Collaboration leads to an increase in interdependencies that the maladaptive response seeks to reduce. The system-as-a-whole gets larger in members' minds, imposing further burdens on cognition. A dilemma emerges; individuals and groups can feel that their sense-making is threatened by an overload of information, before they have developed the capacity to process it. Intervention to support cognition during the development of collaboration seems vital.

I pictured the flow as under-bounded and interconnected swirls of energy (see Figure 1). McCann and Selsky (1997, p. 192) provided a clue to a consulting intervention to help contain the flow. When an environment becomes grossly overloaded, but before hyperturbulence becomes endemic, they argue that partitioning or segmenting the environment into domains will occur. This occurs to protect and foster the limited adaptive capacity. The potential danger in this partitioning process is that it might increase the gaps in adaptive capacity between groups, unless the potentially dysfunctional consequences of their interdependencies with others can be minimized.

My working hypothesis was that an intervention into the "organization in the mind" (Armstrong, 2006, p. 79) might bring greater focus to the transitional organizational form, and help to draw the organization out of its retreat from this task. To partition or define the functional domains in the transitional form more clearly might provide containment and support the development of leadership to help clarify the remaining questions and issues. It could build broader and deeper involvement, with representation and buy-in from the countries, enhancing integration. It could help to clarify critical interfaces, and also support the definition of, and work on, interdependencies.

By offering a new shape, the system or organization-in-the-mind could be reified and verified with members, and a design for the new transitional organization be brought into collective awareness and support members in re-engaging within a new organizational form. The transitional shape needed to contain but not reduce organizational complexity. The objective was to avoid being stuck, while increasing adaptive capacity.

The difficulty with any transitional organizational form is that it is designed to reshape many dimensions of the system, disrupting the political landscape and its power structures, with the resulting threats to roles, identities, relationships, and status.

In what follows I illustrate how I have used aspects of these theoretical perspectives of organization to ground my experience and inform my thinking and practice in turbulent and hyper-turbulent conditions.

Selected interventions and outcomes using visual metaphors

During one of my informal "have you got a minute?" chats with the head of the technology team, I drew the following picture of the organizational hyper-turbulence I perceived (Figure 1).

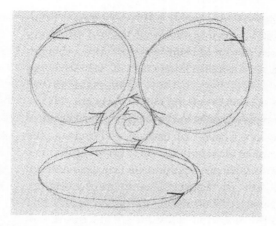

Figure 1.   The four rotating swirls.

The four rotating swirls each represented a broad functional area of the emerging business. Technology is the platform on which all else rests, supporting the two core competencies of the business. These are all interconnected by the look and feel of the design function that linked the competencies to the end consumer. The swirling represented my sense of organizational hyper-turbulence, each swirl interconnected and energizing others like vortices in a complex storm. The image immediately resonated with him. At that moment I sensed we had the beginnings of something significant. It struck me that the diagram resembled Edvard Munch's painting *The Scream.*

The Scream seemed to capture the emotional sentiment within the project team at the time, a sense of organizational angst. I hung a poster of this picture on the wall of the project office. It immediately raised knowing looks as if it indicated or represented some kind of nadir. A shared experience of *The Scream* emerged in the central team through humour and dialogue around the picture. It helped the central team process difficult elements of their experience. It also helped people to reflect on their own emotional state individually and made it all right to acknowledge and own those feelings. Central team members became aware of my observations and began to see them for themselves. They picked up the terms "turbulence" and "vortex" and they became part of the symbolic language within the team.

This was a first step in a complex responsive process (Stacey, 2003, p. 329). The diagram and picture generated conversations about previously unspoken thoughts and feelings. These conversations spread in a complex pattern of interactions in the team and across the wider organization. (This complex responsive process was repeated in subsequent stages of intervention. Each subsequent visual metaphor became an attractor of attention within the organizational complexity. A focal point around which to develop, enhance, and extend shared understanding.)

This validation of the image of the rotating swirls gave it credibility and some transformational power. I sensed it could be turned into something others could see, discuss, and help to adapt. This abstract and outline shape encompassed the dynamics I had observed between groups; all of the interfaces where the difficult interdependent dynamics occurred appeared in this metaphor. Visual representations of organization were not prevalent in CommCo Organization charts showing hierarchy were available on a central intranet, but only illustrated a small portion of the organization on the screen at any one time. Seeing organization as a whole, and relatedness between parts, was new. I initiated and led a process of brainstorming the high-level interdependent issues. Using the underlying shape of the four swirls with the functional groups, we placed Post-it notes describing issues in rough positions around the swirls and drew lines between them to describe the interconnections. Others in the office were curious and joined in the conversation. The diagram became a conversational tool helping to contain complex ideas and interrelationships. Conversations were changed in the process (for a fuller elaboration of the use and power of changing conversations in organizations, see Shaw [2002]). Placing the issues on this interdependency diagram helped to anchor those issues against the relentless flow. The mood changed as people saw interconnections, the "system-as-a-whole" and its issues, for the first time and with clarity.

While participating in a large team meeting, a refinement of this metaphor emerged that built on the key elements of the swirls diagram. It also linked to my hypothesis about blurred boundaries around the groups in the emergent transitional organization and my sense of collective withdrawal from dialogue. The current organizational form and its dynamics stifled any movement towards greater clarity of the issues and hampered work to resolve them. Country territories remained embedded in their silos with views about what was best for their operation, not the enterprise as a whole.

Metaphors work to make the groups and their interfaces clearer and locate interdependent issues in their meaningful locations so that links between the "becoming accountable" groups are clearer. This in turn helps to define the interdependent input or output between groups, a necessary step in building a picture of the system-as-a-whole for verification by the wider organization. It also has the potential to illustrate the need for clearer accountabilities and responsibilities. This was a sensitive step, defended against as described earlier. Therefore, I took an indirect route to illustrate the gap and facilitate thinking about the implications.

I scribbled the emerging visualization in my notebook. Within hours the rough, hand-drawn diagram had been photocopied and had become a focus of conversation within the change team. The diagram (Figure 2) sparked new conversations and generated a further complex responsive process of dialogue, interaction, and interpretation.

The visual metaphor prompted thinking about the relative position of the project board. Concepts of the "organization-in-the-

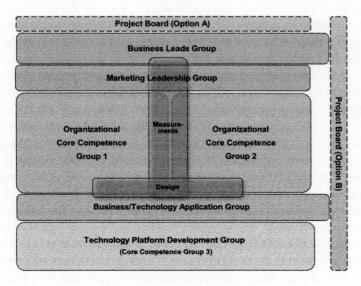

Figure 2.   A visual metaphor of the groups and their interfaces.

mind" seemed to differ. Some saw its position at the top of the diagram, the highest hierarchical group. Others saw it running down
the side, with two key interfaces to business strategy and technology expertise. In this visual dilemma lay an important issue within
the organization.

The interface between the expertise in business strategy and
technology strategy was not effective enough. "Why can't anybody
tell us what they want to do?" was a soul-searching lament from the
technology team. The solution was to form a new interface group,
the Business and Technology Application Group, with broad representation from those "trapped" by this seemingly circular issue.
The visual metaphor illustrated the need and relational place for
this group (at the interface between the core competence groups)
and it was quickly formed. Again, the refined visual metaphor stimulated discussion and engagement and quickly entered circulation
within the change team. It became an object for members to look at
and converse about together. It furthered shared understanding
about a new transitional organizational form.

Another organizational insight concerned work group membership and representation. Was the change team representative in
each of these groups the most appropriate person? Was the link to
the in-country representative at the right level in the organization?
Naming the individuals threw up a valuable insight; it was unclear.
Placing individual accountability and responsibility for key issues
emerging in the interdependencies diagram was not a clear-cut
process. The need for clearer accountabilities was apparent. Seeing
it in this way, as a system-as-a-whole facing challenge and change,
raised the issues in a collective and less threatening way. A collective will to clarify the issues emerged. This movement, while
supportive and seemingly progressive, immediately raised the
spectre of changes in the landscape of politics and power. There
were calls for a clearer governance and decision-making framework
from senior levels.

To support the emergence and development of these interdependent groups, I developed a one-page, open-systems framework for each of the key groups depicted in Figure 2. The
framework comprised many boxes in which to list key information
to discuss, agree, and share between groups; the group's objectives
and key accountabilities; key unanswered questions to focus on;

named representatives and roles; interdependencies with other groups in terms of inputs and outputs; key interfaces and interdependent issues; critical success factors; decision-making authority of the group; what the escalation route was for conflict resolution, etc. This framework was taken up by the central Business Lead and used widely within the central change team to brainstorm, refine, agree, and allocate key issues and accountabilities to the groups. There was urgency in this work, as if energy had been released where previously it was blocked.

A draft summary of the diagrams, metaphors, and frameworks was sent out to leaders around the organization with accompanying explanations. Then followed a two-week consultation and discussion period. There was a sense of the vortex dispersed far and wide, away from the central change team. It was clear that many side discussions were occurring. Teleconferences were offered, arranged, and taken up, and provided discussion forums and means of giving feedback. I felt that these provided containment, as previously disparate and dispersed groups heard each other's discussions, sensed agreement, and moved towards a more collaborative transitional state. (Feedback comments during this process included: "It's a good co-operation document"; "It's really helped pull the detail of this together"; "It's a rather complex structure, but I think it's the only way"; "We'll evolve it, refine it as we go along".)

In parallel, my attention turned to information processing in the transitional organization. There was a sequence or flow, in part towards the Project Board, where key decisions would need to be made, but also emanating from the various groups, needing multiple points of integration. It again seemed necessary to allow information to flow as freely as possible and allow sense-making and decisions at the appropriate group level.

As I socialized my thinking about this process through conversations with the Business Leads group, an organization-wide phenomenon emerged that called for "Project Tuesday", a dedicated day that the "becoming accountable" staff would blank out in their diaries and devote only to this project. A weekly meeting was set up, with an agenda structure that followed the flow described above. This was felt to be a major leap forward by all. People who had been too "busy" or withdrawn to engage were now eagerly calling for 20% of their diaries to be cohesively focused on the issues, together.

Here was a complex responsive process unfolding. The containment provided by the visual metaphors and the initial drawing of four interlinked swirls had developed into open-systems frameworks, reviewed and engaged with across the organization, resulting in a dramatic turnaround in engagement and dialogue.

Conceptualizing the system in a state of hyperturbulence focused my attention on the passive maladaptive responses; superficial dialogue, group withdrawal, lack of engagement across organizational interfaces, and superficial accountabilities and responsibilities. It prompted my thinking of the need to stimulate adaptive activity through deeper dialogue to clarify the issues and build shared understanding; greater engagement across organizational interfaces; supporting collaboration and greater integration through an open-systems approach. It also helped the central change team become mindful of lateral relations, relative adaptive capacities, and the factors that may be affecting this, such as skills, experience, resources, and the affect of systems psychodynamics.

On the use and usefulness of visual metaphors

A visual metaphor is an analogue, a thing comparable in some way to the organizational setting and its issues. The swirls diagram (Figure 1) captured the essence of the troublesome situation: that in a system undergoing significant and rapid changes, many interlinked issues lead to dynamics between parts or sub-elements of the system that threaten to overwhelm the system-as-a-whole. Visual metaphors are the result of mindful sense-making in the here-and-now; of watching the issues arise in the organizational setting, of processing projective identifications with those data, and making cause and effect interpretations. The visual metaphors are my projections representing an interpretation of the organizational issues I perceived. They are a reification of that personal sense making, a representation or map, but not reality. The visual metaphor helps to represent, reduce, and simplify the amount of data to be processed, while retaining enough complexity to make it relevant and engaging. It needs to be "representative enough" of the key themes to be conveyed from the organizational analysis. If it is representative enough, it becomes an attractor of organizational attention and useful for focusing and stimulating work on the issues represented. It does not have to be "right" to be useful. There is no right answer, only subjective interpretation. It is conveying subjective experience, which differs between members. The fact that others interpret the situation differently, would draw a different metaphor, or derive different understanding from the metaphor, is part of its transformational power.

Early sharing of the visual metaphor with the client tests the consultant's initial thinking, supports the early stage formulation and shaping, and builds trust between consultant and client and among client groups across organizational interfaces. Keeping it in rough form, letting it be played with, sustaining it as a malleable, flexible, and adaptable notion for as long as possible, helps to reduce resistance as the ideas embed and the metaphor spreads.

The metaphors were catalysts around which members could gather, converse, and develop a deeper shared understanding. They were containing, holding points of discussion, while enabling interlinked elements to be recognized in relation to the point being discussed. Visual metaphors gave the issues a sense of place in relation to one another.

The catalytic effect of the metaphors moved the system forward to the next "sticking-point". There was a sense of a lurch forward through an organizational impasse. How do we relate to one another in this new configuration? In this way, the metaphor is a useful tool for overcoming organizational defences. It presents complex information in a less threatening or overwhelming way, and thus stimulates engagement and organizational sense-making. The lurch through the sticking point led quickly to multiple concurrent calls for a governance and decision-making framework. There is a need to be highly responsive to these evolving and emergent needs, to keep a complex responsive process of sense-making vibrant and active. As consultant, it was possible to sense the need in advance of it being asked and to have begun formulating a response. Having something "good enough" ready for that next step, after the organization had begun its sense-making of the current step, was powerful in keeping momentum, and containing and diffusing potential difficulties before they became significant.

On consulting and use of self as instrument

Use of "self as instrument" in these turbulent conditions warrants reflection. As a participant in a hyperturbulent system, I am potentially vulnerable to the impact of systems psychodynamics as much as other organizational members. Having an external role is helpful, if not vital, in enabling effective work "on the boundary" of the system. Not too far in to be subsumed, and not too far out to lose touch with the organizational dynamics.

There is always the possibility of the consultant mirroring the internal dynamics of an organization. In this case study, potential passive maladaptive responses were for the consultant: to be subsumed by a part of the system and dissociate from others; not to challenge dialogue but stay within boundaries to avoid complexity and difficult questions. During my early discussions with the client, I was quietly told that a challenging style did not work: "We just go with the flow around here". Any interventions, therefore, needed to take into account the prevailing culture and the organizational defences at work in the system.

Note

1. This chapter is a registered activity as part of 'Refreshing the Tavistock Institute's Intellectual Traditions'.

References and bibliography

Alderfer, C. P. (1980). Consulting to underbounded systems. In: C. P. Alderfer & C. L. Cooper (Eds.), *Advances in Experiential Processes, Volume 2* (pp. 267–295). Wiley.

Alderfer, C. P., & Smith, K. K. (1982). Studying intergroup relations embedded in organizations. *Administrative Science Quarterly, 27*: 35–65.

Angyal, A. (1941). *Foundations for a Science of Personality*. Cambridge, MA: Harvard University Press.

Armstrong, W. G. (2006). *Organization in the Mind: Psychoanalysis, Group Relations and Organizational Consultancy*. London: Karnac.

Baburoglu, O. (1988). The vortical environment: the fifth in the Emery–Trist levels of organizational environments. *Human Relations, 41*(3): 181–210.

Emery, F. E., & Trist, E. L. (1965). The causal texture of organizational environments. *Human Relations, 18*(1): 21–32.

Emery, F. (1977). Passive maladaptive strategies. In: E. Trist & H. Murray (1997) *The Social Engagement of Social Science, A Tavistock Anthology: Volume Three: The Socio-ecological Perspective* (pp. 99–114). Pennsylvania: University of Pennsylvania Press.

Menzies Lyth, I. (1988). The functioning of social systems as a defence against anxiety. A report on the study of the nursing service of a general hospital. In: *Containing Anxiety in Institutions* (pp. 43–99). London: Free Association.

Miller, E. J., & Rice, A. K. (1990). Task and sentient systems and their boundary controls. In: E. Trist & H. Murray (Eds.), *The Social Engagement of Social Science, Volume One: The Socio-psychological Perspective* (pp. 259–271). London: Free Association.

McCann, J., & Selskey, J. (1997). Hyperturbulence and the emergence of type V environments. In: E. Trist & H. Murray (Eds.), *The Social Engagement Of Social Science, Volume Three: The Socio-ecological Perspective* (pp. 185–202). Philadelphia, PA : University of Pennsylvania Press.

Shaw, P. (2002). *Changing Conversations in Organizations: A Complexity Approach to Change.* Oxford: Routledge.

Stacey, R. (2003). *Strategic Management and Organizational Dynamics. The Challenge of Complexity* (4th edn). Harlow: FT/Prentice Hall.

Sydow, J., & Windeler, A. (1998). Organizing and evaluating inter-firm networks: a structurationist perspective on network processes and effectiveness. *Organization Science, 9*(3): 265–284.

Trist, E. (1983). Referent organizations and the development of inter-organizational domains. In: E. Trist & H. Murray (Eds.), *The Social Engagement of Social Science Volume Three: The Socio-ecological Perspective* (pp. 170–184). Philadelphia, PA: University of Pennsylvania Press.

Weick, K. E. (1995). *Sensemaking in Organizations.* London: Sage.

Weick, K. E. (2001). *Making Sense of the Organization.* Oxford: Blackwell.

CHAPTER FOUR

Power dynamics of expertise and containment in the process of hiring and being hired

Veronika Grueneisen and Karen Izod

Introduction

Descriptions of consultancy–client relationships in the literature often refer to a two-way fit between players: e.g., doctor–patient (Schein, 1987, pp. 24–29) or a relationship based on contribution, 50–50 collaboration, pair of hands, expert (Block, 1981). In this chapter, we are concerned to look at the dynamic interchanges between contractors and providers of consultancy relationships, recognizing that at different times in the consultancy relationship different dynamics will dominate, and that these are indicative of emergent power relationships and the extent to which each player can manage personal or organizational risk.

In our early conceptualization of these themes, we began by identifying experiences of seeking consultancy that, for some reason, had not been able to meet our needs. Both of us had had encounters with consultants to whom we were attracted because of their (apparent) brilliance. However, in these consultations we experienced this brilliance as attacking our own ability to think and to be in touch with our own good enough competence. Thinking through these experiences together, we began to wonder how this had occurred and what the dynamics between consultant and contractor might be whereby something initially perceived as desirable could not develop into a sustaining relationship.

In discussing these contracting experiences, we explored something of the situation of consultants wanting to get work. We saw consultants as having their consultancy domain in mind, and relating to their expertise as primarily something to sell. The consultants' expertise is a constitutive element in how they present themselves to a contractor: this is what they do and know about, and want to be hired for. At this stage, ideas of providing containment for the client is likely to be secondary, and might, in any case, not be evident.

But this way of thinking about their work and what they have to offer has pitfalls. When consultants set off like this, they can (1) present themselves in a way which makes the contractor feel denigrated in their own competence; (2) ignore the contractor's (possibly as yet unsurfaced) need for containment.

If consultants set off by giving attention to containment, however, they run the risk that their expertise will not be noticed, that containment is not "visible" for their contractor as a skill and part of their competence. To the extent that the consultant is aware of this dilemma, it can interrupt and paralyse their capacity to act. Where the consultant is unaware, it can lead to mismatches and, eventually, failure in the consultation process.

Moving on, we came to think about the position of the contractor and the needs and competences they bring to the process. Making a decision to contract a consultant often means an awareness that something is felt and identified as lacking, or that something new needs to be created for which different resources and perspectives are needed. This is often thought about in terms of expertise; particular skills or attributes that can be brought to bear on the issues at stake. Our experience is that contractors may see themselves as in need only of the consultants' specific expertise, and look first for their domain. Expressing a need for consultation can be difficult, and especially so in an organizational culture where there is an expectation that all the necessary expertise should reside within one's self or the organization.

Definitions of the consultant's expertise then needs to "fit" with the contractor's competencies so as to be sufficiently different from what the contractors themselves have to offer. This may seduce contractors into overlooking or ignoring that they themselves might have the very expertise they are looking for, but which might not be available because some organizational process blocks them. Looking for "an expertise" instead of "an engagement offering containment" can prevent contractors paradoxically from getting where they want to. Indeed, it may be the case that it is not so much an expertise that the contractor is lacking, but someone helping them to identify what prevents them from making good enough use of their ordinarily good competence. Therefore, the consultant's expertise can be both wanted and not wanted, both helpful and not helpful. In order not to create a mismatch at an early stage of the consulting cycle, it is helpful for both contractors and consultants to get an idea of what containment might mean in consultation—not only as an offer of consultants to contractors, but also of contractors to consultants.

In this chapter, we explore the idea that, from the beginning, the consultant and the contractor are mutual and inescapable sources of anxiety for the other. This phenomenon creates delicate power differentials between consultant and contractor, which need to be both acknowledged and managed during contracting. In the process, it is inevitable that elements of personal and organizational risk are encountered. We will also explore what it may mean for a successful contracting process to keep both sides (consultant and contractor) and their mutuality, as well as both aspects (expertise and containment), in mind.

Definitions

Expertise. We are defining the term "expertise" as relating to an ordinarily good capacity to think and intervene with a client system in relation to a particular problem or set of challenges. We might expect that this capacity is supported by related experiences in other client systems, together with the ability to access a number of theoretical models that can illustrate one's thinking. This is the technology of consulting: the capacity to bring in a number of methodologies and tools to make a difference to the problem, and which results in the consultant's claim to their domain. The technology for the client, to attend to and make use of their organizational and environmental capacity in the service of its primary task, represents a similar expertise for the client system.

Containment. The term "containment" stems from Bion (1970). It is taken from a concept of early infant–mother communication, connected to the capacity to hold the infant in mind as a thinking, feeling, and separate being, and is the basis for a development of reflection (Fonagy & Target, 2005). In terms of containment in organizational consulting, we mean by this that containment is needed when there is a breakdown in functioning in role in relation to task, stemming from anxiety or frustration. Managing such anxiety or frustration can enable the client or consultant to bring more possibilities into their thinking, and so extend the range of options that are available for them. This may be alleviated structurally, i.e., with contracts and procedures and through a process of disentangling (Benjamin, 1998, p. xiv) from the emotions that limit functioning and creativity. This containing process is rarely evident when it is in place, but is realized and felt much more in its absence.

We have begun to conceptualize these elements of expertise and containment as offering different constellations of dynamics at work within the contracting process. Conceptualized as dyads, we are proposing that both contractor and consultant are complementary to each other in relation to both expertise and containment. When one has a need, and the other has an offer, this constitutes a power differential that can be noticed and managed. We see these dynamics as operating within each dyad. Neither competence nor containment are sufficient in themselves, and, while existing independently, they work in relation to each other —each dyad, therefore, exists in a relatedness to the others. This is illustrated in Figure 1, and expanded upon in our case examples and discussion. Working through difficulties encountered in hiring or being hired may be helped by identifying where the consultant–contractor pair is in relation to these dynamics at any given time. (We acknowledge that the use of the word "dyad' may imply singular entities, and that consultants may also work as teams and in systems, as do clients. Our examples relate to single consultants.)

Dyad 1	Dyad 2
Contractor requires/needs expertise Consultant has expertise and wants to sell it	Contractor has expertise and needs to access it Consultant needs to elicit expertise in client

Dyad 3	Dyad 4
Contractor requires/needs containment Consultant has the capacity to contain	Consultant needs containment to work Client has the capacity to contain

Figure 1.   Dynamics of expertise and containment in the process of hiring and being hired.

Examples from practice

Dyad 1: Contractor requires/needs expertise; consultant has expertise and wants to sell it

Wanting to create a website for my (KI) consultancy practice, I engaged an IT consultant whose company brought together both the technical and creative aspects of website development. My hopes were that through this relationship I would be able to create a content to describe my consulting activities, and the consultant would be able to craft this into an attractive and accessible website. I had been impressed by websites that his company had previously produced for independent professionals, and, although fees were expensive, he seemed to provide a level of expertise appropriate to the added value I imagined would arise.

This was a consultancy that ultimately proved unsuccessful in terms of our ability to negotiate, create and maintain a relationship that would enable both of us to access our expertise and ordinary competence for a joint task. The "lure of brilliance" offered through the expertise of the consultancy did not prepare me for an encounter in which I felt blinded by the consultant's technical knowledge, and unable to relate to the templates through which I needed to prepare my material. For his part, I was aware that the consultant was unable to understand the impasse that we reached; that making statements about my consulting practice and the market images that that would convey was anxiety-producing work for which I needed some help. As the consultant became more and more proficient in his own domain, I became less and less able, more exhausted, and unable to retain and respond to what he had to say.

Expertise and competence

In this encounter, the consultant was able to convey the expertise of his company in a results-orientated and compelling way. But it was clear that we differed in the extent to which we saw this as a joint endeavour. I had envisaged the process as one in which both our competences were needed, and I could quickly sense my own unwillingness to be a passive partner. I could not be "done to" in the sense of fitting in easily to the consultant's requirements of me; perhaps because this would have meant confrontation with an aspect of uneasiness about my own sense of competence in the vast field of consulting, and the risk that I was taking in going public about it. It is likely that this unease helped to make the consultant's brilliance so seductive.

A mutual attunement between us was lacking, such that my usually good-enough skills of presenting myself and my work to others, of writing texts and coming up with ideas, started to fail. I became increasingly alienated by the language, structures, and norms of the website template that I was being offered. Without this level of contribution from me, the consultant was unable to function. He needed me to be able to hold on to a sense of what I wanted, and my own professional capacities, in order for him to access his undoubted skills. At some level, the consultant was unable to engage with the competence of my organization, or link with the nature of risk that the enterprise represented.

The power dynamics show most clearly in the shifting emotions and states of mind encountered within the dyad. There will never be an equal power. Instead, it appears crucial to recognize where power resides at different moments, and with view to different aspects of the process.

In the mismatch between the IT consultant and KI, the consultant appears to her quite powerful through the expertise his organization has shown in their web products. Only in the process of working together does KI become aware of her need to have her anxieties contained, anxieties that she experiences around presenting her consulting practice in the electronic space. Possibly, the very fact of a felt powerlessness in relation to the consultant, due to his special skills, makes it important for her not to be treated as a passive partner but to be included into a collaborative process and have their respective expertises combined in creating the website together. However, the consultant tries to exert his expertise by requiring her to fit her statements into the norms of his website template. The more obvious it becomes that KI is too frustrated to do this, the more the consultant becomes dependent on her, which results in him losing his power of expertise.

Personal and organizational risk emerges in attempting the task and coming into contact with how it impinges on our emotions and abilities. In this case, the risk for KI of "going public" about her consultancy became strongly associated with the development of the website. As a contracting client, it seems likely that we under-estimate and devalue our needs for help, and the containment that requires, since it shows so little of our own brilliance. It does seem easier to ask for someone's skills when it does not touch upon on our own belief in our own capacities. This can be a humbling experience, in which the competence of the consultant can be threatening.

Depending on what is at stake for the consultant and their orga-nization, it may be possible to be drawn into over-statements of competences, and suggestions of possible outcomes, through a process of spin. This is often a response to the client's expressed need for competence in the face of anxiety. It runs the risk of the consultant reinforcing their own sense of competence, and, if successful, believing in their own narcissistic brilliance. The lure of brilliance privileges a power-based relationship, the power of knowing, which is seen as preferable to that of power being located in the relationship, in the capacity to help people think and gener-ate conditions for change.

The task for the consultant here is to recognize anxiety as a central element in engagement, and to support the client in manag-ing those anxieties. In this scenario, the consultant might have been helped in this task by holding on to the notion that knowledge, skills, and resources do reside in the contractor and their organiza-tion, but, for the moment, are diminished by the developmental task that is being attempted. Skill will lie in the capacity to surface and identify levels of existing knowledge and competence, and the organizational forces that are working to diminish them, or to render them insufficient.

Dyad 2: Contractor has competence and needs to access it; consultant needs to elicit competence in client

> I (KI) was commissioned to provide consultancy to a Social Care Service experiencing difficulty in attracting and retaining staff, and subsequently unable to allocate high-risk cases. The service was located in an area with high levels of need, combined with low levels of community resources. Poor staffing levels both added to, and were a symptom of, the demands that this area consistently faced. The stated purpose for the consultation was to help the organization access and strengthen its own capacities to manage, following a period of exhaustion.

> Three key client systems were involved, each needing to have a sense of ownership of the dilemmas, and their potential solutions. I was brought in not only for my consulting skills, but also for my known managerial resilience in the face of similar scenarios, when I had worked in a similar field. Indicators were that the organization needed to find its own ordinary good competence, rather than be faced with external expertise.

Expertise and containment

This was an organization that was ordinarily competent, but in which that competence was being reduced, indeed, felt attacked, by numerous processes: staff sickness, new procedures, organizational restructuring. These were evident in the demands of the primary task (the safeguarding and care of vulnerable individuals), which had brought them to the point of asking for consultancy, and also in the interplay between the three organizational systems, all competing for the validity of their own diagnoses. It was essential for me to hold on to and mirror the belief that good enough people were appointed to do the job, and not to get caught up in the single realities I heard about individuals that could undermine the complexity of this system. I also needed to not to let myself be drawn into some narcissistic brilliance in the fantasy that I could do it better.

In a system where many players felt guilty that they had not been able to effect better change, how they perceived my own competence became troublesome. It was impossible for me to function without finding a way to establish and hold a position as a competent professional, but one who could be fallible. Indeed, early on, I did encounter myself as inept, with painful reminders of early work in my career emerging to unnerve me. It was an experience of being in touch with the kind of resilience that was needed to manage reputation, and to persevere in the face of what seemed a tyrannical observable primary task, that of not making mistakes.

In turn, I needed to elicit sufficient competence from the organization so that they could manage their relationship with me. Ultimately, this was available in the competence of the contract, in taking care that it was crafted in a way that could support the work from its multiple perspectives. Without this as a stake in the ground, it would not have been possible to work at any kind of edge, such was the shifting ground in the dynamics. Eventually, it was possible to access the competence of the system as a whole through a strongly containing measure to get all the key players in a neutral space, and offering a thematic, more educative agenda for discussion. Through this framework, individuals could associate to the issues at hand, in a thoughtful and deliberative way, and the multiplicity of perspectives could begin to be appreciated.

In KI's consultation with the Social Care Service, *the power differential* initially lies in her wanting to have the assignment over against some of her potential clients having doubts about her competence and the need for a consultant, anyway. Part of the danger for KI in role is to let herself be seduced into the role of a colleague who is powerful but potentially degrading for her client, a colleague who is needed because she knows better. Instead, she succeeds in opening up ways for members of the organization to re-access their own resources and capacities. Interestingly, KI finds access to her own power in negotiating a contract in such a way that it allows her to gather together members of the three different systems involved in an educational event, designed to allow members to make use of, rather than defend themselves against, the inevitable multiple perspectives involved, so that they are able to find new solutions.

Personal and organizational risk is encountered here in a mutual and enacted process. One risk for this organization is in acknowledging that it can and will make mistakes. This is an almost impossible concept to bring to the surface, with fears of the consequences for vulnerable individuals, and is much easier to locate in the procedures and restructurings than in the decisions that are actually made about specific clients. The risk for KI was in making her own fallibility available to the client, and running the risk of being rejected by them as incompetent, rather than being able to work with fallibility as an essential component of the work—that you cannot guarantee that you will get it right.

As consultants, we need to grasp what it is about the nature of the enterprise that contributes to these situations and makes demands on its competence, that then feels, and is, so difficult to acknowledge. Depending on the organization, this might include the tyranny of the production line, 24/7 residential care, or the need to constantly innovate and produce new knowledge. Trying to create some space between the organization and its enterprise can allow for some reflection about the demands on competence that can feel so threatening.

Dyad 3: Contractor requires/needs containment; consultant has the capacity to contain

One of my (VG) experiences of being hired was a role consultation with a manager of an organization comprising 2000 employees, with different units for older people, originally owned by the city. The manager had been responsible for making the organization economically independent, and had achieved this within five years. His current reason for contacting me was a decision of his board to install a management colleague whom he had not chosen and was heavily opposed to, an event that he understood and suffered from as a really very bad failure. He came asking for help with working together with this colleague (he had not been able to work well with her predecessor) and with the board, especially the president, who had disappointed him by taking this—in his eyes disastrous—decision.

My difficulty with this consultation was that the client did not seem to be able to work with what I had to offer. He appeared in no way prepared to reflect on his way of working with his colleague, his board, or his president. He showed an attitude that is described in German as "wash my fur but don't make me wet".

In one of the sessions, he was trying to prepare a day seminar with his middle managers and his management colleague. He did not know how to define their roles respectively, or how to speak with her about it. Whatever I suggested to look at in order to clarify his emotions and his thinking in view of the task, he rejected. We both seemed to get more and more helpless, and I suggested a break in which I offered refreshments and left the room in order to think about what was going on. Only then was I able to understand my feelings of utter uselessness in respect of countertransference (reflection of his emotional state of mind in myself). When, after our break, I asked him whether he might feel helpless and useless, he agreed with great relief, he became able to think of a strategy, and commented on what I said to him that he had thought of this, "anyway".

Expertise and competence

This incident helped me to understand that I had been expecting my client to want my containment in the form of offering my expertise instead of helping him to access his own. As consultants, we may be inclined to forget the extent to which our clients are competent and need to be respected and acknowledged in their own expertise. In fact, doing this, explicitly or implicitly, can be a containing function just because, mostly, consultants are invited in when clients are less sure of their own capabilities and need acknowledgement in order to be able to get out of their stuckness.

In the above example, the manager was desperately in need of this kind of acknowledgement in order to be able to take in anything of what I might have to say. As long as I did not understand this side of him, he could not listen to what I had to say, as anything he might have taken in felt to him as proving his neediness, which, in his mind, meant his incompetence.

In the role consultation, the containment this client could make use of consisted in my suggesting a break, offering refreshment to the client, trying to think, in a separate room, about my depression, and working it out as my countertransference. Suggesting to my client that he might feel helpless in his organization allowed him to be able to think again, creatively, about his work.

In situations like this, we as consultants need to remind ourselves that we are not consulting to individuals, but to systems. Linking us as a pair with the nature of the enterprise, which was about disability, might have helped me to confront myself with, and acknowledge, my disability to work with him and would have opened up the ability to acknowledge the systemic influence and work with it.

This consultation also made me aware of my need to be contained myself, by a minimum of acknowledgement, through my client. Had he been able to show some appreciation, I might have been able to function better. As he could not, I looked for shadow consultation, i.e., containment, through a consultant for myself, in order to get in touch again with my expertise and my competence, including my capacities to contain.

As to *power dynamics* in this role consultation, VG assumes the commissioning manager to be quite powerful and competent due to his achievement in his organization. Possibly, this leads her to increase her wish to prove "really helpful", i.e., play out her expertise. However, he wrestles with feelings of powerlessness against his board and his new colleague. In fact, he is structurally dependent, and cannot play out his power against the board. Politically, the board wields its power against the manager, by excluding him from their decision-making in relation to their appointment, and thereby encourages his resistance.

Possibly, already in this decision, some of the nature of the enterprise determines the power dynamics in the organization, i.e., the inclination of the board to "know better" and impose a solution on its most important manager that he cannot accept. In a similar way nursing staff may impose care on the disabled residents, who then feel disempowered and drawn into resistance against the people who are there to take care of them. This dynamic then takes hold of the consultation: the manager cannot experience VG's input as enrichment of his capacities, but experiences it as a threat to his professional and personal integrity, as can happen with people with disabilities who thrive if given space to play out their abilities instead of being confined to their possible need for support.

Personal and organizational risk is encountered here in the humility required, in both consultant and contractor, to understand that one's competence is not all that is needed in managing and consulting to human dilemmas within organizations. Many things occur about which one has only partial knowledge and over which one has little control. We do not know what led the board to make the decision it did in its controversial appointment, but assume that the nature of the enterprise in some way required something different in the face of its overt success. It might be the case that achieving financial independence for the institution provided the catalyst for conflict in terms of its politics and ideology, and that the board now needed to secure its functioning in a different way, through new and different approaches. This comes to represent the kind of primary risk that Hirschhorn (1999) speaks of when a new strategic direction is needed, and is experienced by some as a "put down" rather than the enrichment to the organization that is intended.

Dyad 4: Consultant needs containment to work; client has the capacity to contain

In adult education, hiring external colleagues for training and development seminars was one of my (VG's) main tasks. When I was new in this job, I was more concerned with my own emotional situation, looking for containment for myself. I felt insecure with my role as a trainer and in my concept of what participants should learn. I was trying to deepen their political and educational understanding of their work and felt that I needed to deepen this understanding myself. This is why I was looking for colleagues who would bring the same competence to a seminar that I tried to bring, so as to add to what I felt was insufficient about myself. In fact, I think that this was an appropriate strategy, at this time of my career, as the trainer needs to look after himself first in order to function well enough as a container for the group.

In later years, I felt safer with what I had to offer, and began to look for colleagues who would bring competencies that I did not have so as to enlarge the offer of the trainer team for participants. Then, the way I offered containment as a contracting client was around a clear structure: my prospective colleagues had to know what I wanted from them, what my conditions and resources were, what I wanted them to do and what I wanted to do myself. I felt it important to clarify for them (and for myself) in which way their competencies would fit in with the task and my needs for working together on the task.

I had to try to find out—usually on the phone—about the other person's expertise, their approach to learning, the repertoire of methods they were used to and willing to offer and how they fitted with my approach, their experience with, and willingness to work in, a team and under a team leader. I had to make clear what my interest in their competence was and offer space for them to use it at work. I had to grant task, time, and territory for the team, structure our work, offer and fix dates and deadlines, etc.

Expertise and competence

My colleagues in adult education needed to demonstrate their expertise and competence and I had to be able to recognize it as such in order for me to feel contained. At the same time, I was dependent on my colleagues' containment for myself in role: in any group situation focusing on experiential learning it is easy to get involved more than is appropriate for the leadership task. Having a colleague around who shared the leadership task in the group meant that, when I led a session and had to keep the boundary, he or she would be there to keep an eye on the group process, monitor that, and intervene as necessary. My colleagues were dependent on my containment of their anxiety of the unknown they had to manage when I hired them over the phone, not knowing much of the organization I was working with. I gave my containment through detailed information about my organization, my concept and way of working, about what I expected from them in relation to the task, through organizing their stay, and being clear in my leadership role. I was also open to, and appreciative of, their competence, which, in turn, allowed them to access their competence in the seminars. From the consultant's perspective, containment is offered through these elements and also through the capacity to negotiate for a reflecting space to review the work.

Power dynamics in hiring colleagues in adult education come in through VG's power to confine her colleagues' work to the working terms and conditions she set in representing her organization's approach to self-directed learning. However, it was important for the enterprise that she also confined her power if she wanted to get the most out of their expertise. The more space her colleagues got to demonstrate their expertise, the more participants in the seminars could profit and enhance the reputation and, possibly, the market share of the work done by her organization under her leadership. There was, however, a critical boundary that she could not allow a colleague to cross: whatever they did, she needed to be able to see that participants could benefit and learn, and would not be confined to becoming spectators of a hired colleague's expertise, something that would have been damaging for the work and her organization's market position.

Personal and organization risk emerge here for the contractor, in terms of the reputation of the organization, and how to include others who will be able to sustain that identity through their good work. This speaks to an often unsurfaced desire, that of an organization wanting to meet its own needs through its own resources. Being able to provide your own staff allows the fantasy, at least, that there is some control over how staff behave. The risk of what others might do and say is avoided. This is the fantasy that organizations can function as closed systems, rather than needing to interact with others across complex boundaries of identity, purpose, and skill. At an individual level, the risk is more about how to create conditions by which the contractor can lead, and access her competence, knowing paradoxically that, in order to contain the system as a whole, she needs to make space for the containment that her colleagues' competences can offer. We might call this "reciprocal containment".

Discussion

In our exploration of these issues, we have come to think of the task of surfacing and managing the dynamics of expertise and containment as being similar to that of a circus artist, balancing plates upon a stick, attending to them as they begin to wobble and inevitably risk falling.

We suggest, for those engaging and being engaged as consultants, that three things have to be balanced:

- expertise and containment;
- power of contractor and power of consultant;
- personal and organizational risk.

We have described how the need for, and capacity to access features of *expertise and containment* are issues for both contractor and consultant, and, as the case examples suggest, they need to be managed by both as complementarities: that is, existing for both in relation to each other. The challenge for the consultant lies in not being seduced by the explicit request for their expertise, thereby forgetting about the contractor's own expertise and containment capacities. For the contractor commissioning specific expertise, the challenge lies in offering containment rather than control in shaping contractual expectations at a sufficiently early stage, so as to open doors to a more mutually accessible competence. Frequently, we have seen contractors spending considerable time trying to get their consultants to make knowable the unknown, rather than working on what is knowable.

Power differentials manifest in subtle and delicate shifts between contractor and consultant, and are either negotiated or, more likely, assumed and played out. We have described how there can never be an equal power, even when a collaborative stance is intended—rather that power resides with different parties at different moments and in regard to different aspects of the process. In particular, we notice power in the transference–countertransference dynamics, and in the demands and allocation of resources of the organization in relation to its enterprise, which can at times feel tyrannical. *Personal and organizational risk* is encountered as individuals find something in the engagement that challenges their ordinarily good sense of themselves, their competence, and that of their organization. At a personal level, for both consultant and contractor, this can include the risk of trying something new, fear of losing reputation or status, fear of conflict, as well as losing the contract or not bringing it to fruition.

Organizational risk, according to Hirschhorn (1999), occurs at strategic junctures in the life cycle of an organization, where power and politics meet up in choices about the primary task and direction. Who defines this, who gets resources, and who ultimately faces the consequences, are all features that emerge in consulting to change, and provide the bedrock for anxiety in the consulting encounter.

Thinking about organizational risk might scare both consultant and contractor, and brings out the need for good mutual containment. As consultants, we can only ever have partial knowledge of quite what is at stake, and this will be influenced by how we relate to the strategic debates going on, how these touch our own values, and where we identify and locate ourselves within the system as a whole. We also do not know how well our skills and tools can transfer to this situation, and our ability to connect with it. This is a humbling scenario, and a point where some consultants take their leave, before knowing the impact of their interventions. Our view is that the balancing of personal and organizational risks here links back to the capacity of accessing competence as a means of containment. This might be provided by including the identification of a range of choices for the client, as a means of both seeing alternative trajectories arising from choice and providing routes by which specific anxieties might be named and managed.

Ultimately, as consultants, we want to create relationships with clients where competence can be accessed to the benefit of the organization and where mutual learning can take place. Understanding which dyad (Figure 1) the consultant/contractor inhabits at any one time can be helpful in clarifying the dynamics of power and risk that might be at play, and offers ideas about how to move the engagement on through managing the complementary elements of expertise and containment.

References

Benjamin, J. (1998). *Shadow of the Other: Intersubjectivity and Gender in Psychoanalysis*. Routledge.

Bion, W. (1970). *Attention and Interpretation*. London: Tavistock.

Block, P. (1981). *Flawless Consulting: A Guide to Getting Your Expertise Used*. San Diego, CA: Pfeiffer.

Fonagy, P., & Target, M. (2005). Mentalization and the changing aims of child psychoanalysis. In: L. Aron & A. Harris (Eds.), *Relational Psychoanalysis Volume 2: Innovation and Expansion*. Analytic Press.

Hirschhorn, L. (1999). The primary risk. *Human Relations*, 52(1): 5–23.

Schein, E. H. (1987). *Process Consultation, Volume II: Lessons for Managers and Consultants*. Wokingham: Addison-Wesley.

CHAPTER FIVE

Coaching and consulting to small businesses[1]

Karol Szlichcinski and Ian Holder

Introduction

Small enterprises of fewer than fifty people account for almost half of the employment (47%) and more than a third of the turnover (37%) in the UK (Department for Business, Enterprise and Regulatory Reform, 2007). There is huge potential for advisory services that help them perform more effectively.

Small businesses, in particular micro enterprises of fewer than ten people, typically share some common characteristics that stem from:

- the individual psychology of their owners and managers, and their social psychology as small groups of people;
- their interactions with their customers, suppliers, and other features of their environment;
- the processes and technologies they implement to carry out their work.

These shared characteristics contribute to some common business issues and problems faced by many small businesses. In this chapter we review the shared characteristics briefly, and identify some of the resulting issues. We then present three approaches to advising small businesses at key stages in their development that address these common issues. The approaches embody a mindful approach to consulting, albeit to varying degrees.

Individual and social psychology in small businesses

Personality, background, and personal circumstances, in particular the education and employment opportunities to which an individual is exposed, all have a bearing on whether someone chooses to set up their own business (Bridge, O'Neill, & Cromie, 2003). Personality is of interest in that it may influence how a business owner prefers to interact with an adviser.

There is a considerable body of literature on the personality of the entrepreneur, reviewed in Furnham (1992). Operational definitions of an entrepreneur vary, but typically include most, if not all, small business owners. Furnham concludes that five attributes recur regularly in the leading studies of entrepreneurial characteristics: achievement motivation, internal locus of control (i.e., believing that one can control one's own fate), risk-taking propensity, tolerance of ambiguity, and Type-A behaviour. (Type-A behaviour is the combination of competitiveness, high achievement orientation, aggression, impatience, and restlessness that correlates with a high risk of heart disease.) It could be argued that the pressures of setting up and running a business might bring these characteristics to the fore.

There can also be a dark side to the personality of entrepreneurs. Kets de Vries (1977, 1985) claims that entrepreneurs often dislike authority and find it difficult to fit into organizations. He reports a distrust and suspicion of others, coupled with a strong desire for applause. It is likely that people who display these characteristics would be less successful in employment than their peers, and therefore find self-employment a relatively attractive option.

Recent research suggests that people who think they have the skills and experience to start a new business are much more likely to do so than people who do not (GEM, 2001). On one level this is an obvious finding, but it is a reflection of confidence as well as competence: people who start their own businesses tend to be confident that they have the abilities to run them.

Managers of small businesses often report feeling lonely and isolated when considering important decisions relating to strategy or business planning (Gumpert & Boyd, 1984). They complain of a lack of opportunities to discuss their business on a peer-to-peer basis; if they have staff, they feel unable to discuss such matters with them, or think it is inappropriate to do so.

In most small businesses, other members of staff are dependent on the owner–managers:

> It is a characteristic of small business that powers of decision are centralized at the level of the owner–manager, so his or her personality, skills, responsibilities, attitude and behaviour will have a decisive influence on business strategy. (Bridge, O'Neill, & Cromie, 2003, p. 276]

Studies of employer–employee relations in small businesses report that "benevolent autocracy" is common. However, a more fraternal approach is also common, in particular where skilled employees are a scarce resource and need to be valued (Storey, 1994).

Small businesses are by definition small groups of people, and they show patterns of behaviour typical of small groups. Up to about six people, these mimic family dynamics; between six and sixteen or so they are the small group behaviours described by Bion (Turquet, 1974). These "basic assumption" behaviours occur when the emotional needs of small groups outweigh their commitment to achieving their primary task; in small businesses they are most likely to take the form of basic assumption dependency, where group members display excessive dependency on the leader, and fight/flight behaviour, where the group pursues the aim of fighting or fleeing from something or someone.

Interactions with the environment

Large businesses are often able to exert control over their environment through their financial resources, dominance in specific markets, and political influence (Morgan, 1986, pp. 299–315). Depending on the structure of their industry, they may be able to control the companies upstream or downstream in their supply chain. These opportunities are hardly ever available to small businesses. On the contrary, they may be given little freedom of action by larger companies in the supply chain of which they are part; for example, if they are suppliers to the major supermarket chains or motor manufacturers. These small food products' and motor components' suppliers are an extreme example of a more widely shared characteristic: many small businesses are highly dependent on one or two large customers or suppliers.

Not all the common characteristics of the small business environment are malign. National governments and the European Union have recognized the importance of small businesses to economic growth, and small businesses can take advantage of a considerable range of services and support.

Processes and technologies

The very smallest businesses do not need formalized processes. Their processes, and the information to support them, are usually in the heads of the small number of staff members.

As businesses grow, they start to need a few simple common processes, e.g., accounts and staff management, and the technology to support them. However, they often lack the skills to implement them. Of course, a business may also need processes and technologies specific to its particular line of business.

Common business issues and problems

The shared characteristics of small businesses contribute to some common business issues and problems that many of them face, for example:

- how best to grow the business;
- how the business could become less dependent on one or two people as it grows;
- how to ensure that the business stays healthy in a turbulent and uncertain environment;
- how the business could reduce its dependence on one or two customers;
- what processes and technologies the business needs, and how they should be implemented.

They also provide an opportunity to develop consultancy approaches with wide applicability across the small and medium enterprises (SME) sector. In the following sections we present three methodologies that have proved successful at key points in the development of small businesses.

- The decision as to whether to start a business.
- The launch of the first product or a subsequent new product.
- Implementing IT systems.

Our overall approach is to use conventional management consultancy methods where appropriate, but to apply them in a "mindful" way (Germer, 2005), being aware of and accepting the psychological experiences of the small business managers we work with and taking them into account in our consultancy.

Method 1: Business coaching for leaders of small businesses

Context

As two consultants, one with a business, finance, coaching, and counselling background and the other with strategy, marketing, and organizational consulting experience, the authors have formed a team to provide business coaching for leaders of small businesses. Our objective is to help the small business leaders, typically owner–managers, identify how best to develop their businesses. Some of our clients have an existing business; others are currently employed, but want to set up their own business by transferring an existing skill-set or developing a new business concept.

Our approach

Our overall approach is to provide a space combining support and challenge that enables clients to reframe their thinking and review the progress of their businesses and their own progress as individuals over a period of six to nine months. We chose a coaching style because it enables the client to experience change in thinking, have this witnessed, and ground the experience so that the change is affirmed and embedded. We aim to:

- enable the client to clarify ideas and objectives;
- facilitate a full business analysis;
- develop the client's individual and organizational skills and expertise by helping them to reflect on their situation;
- encourage the client to consider work–life balance;
- ensure that the client fully considers life issues and goals in relation to their current stage of life.

The process we have developed has the following components.

- A free initial one-hour fact-finding session. This enables us to understand the client's situation and objectives, and provides the data for us to write a letter proposal for the subsequent coaching engagement. It also provides the client with an introduction to our way of working.
- Further meetings, each of 1.5 hours' duration, at intervals of 2–3 months that enable the client to set objectives and explore individual and organizational needs;
- One or two one-hour telephone coaching sessions during the intervals between meetings.

During the fact-finding session the client meets both coaches and talks about his/her personal and professional experience and motives, the business concept and the current status of the business, and identifies any issues that he/she wants to address in coaching. On the basis of our experience, we also suggest issues that we feel worth addressing, including issues of capitalizing upon successes. We summarize the session towards the end of the hour, and suggest ways of reframing the issues raised. Afterwards, we review our joint experience, draft a letter proposal setting out our understanding of the client's situation, and send it to the client within four days of the meeting.

If the client decides to go ahead with the coaching engagement, the next step is a telephone coaching session with one of us. The client agrees the number and spacing of the meetings, responds to the issues set out in the proposal, and discusses further needs and how their thinking has developed since the meeting.

At subsequent meetings we encourage the client to discuss what has happened during the interval, and identify and review development issues jointly with the client. At the final, completion meeting, we offer an overall summary of the project, and the client discusses their future plans and strategy.

We use Appreciative Inquiry techniques (Cooperrider, Whitney, & Stavros, 2005) to help clients identify where they want to take their business; more specifically, to find out where the strengths and potential of the client lie, where their energy is focused, their vision of their future business, and the practicalities of implementing it.

The presence of two coaches enables one to engage with the client while the other thinks through the business implications of what the client is saying. When the latter coach identifies issues to raise with the client, he takes over the coaching conversation, leaving the other coach to take up the reviewing role. With a small amount of experience we have been able to handle these handovers relatively smoothly.

Where the client has an established business, we also explore any barriers to developing the business to achieve the client's vision. Given the critical role of owner–managers in small businesses, we are alert to situations where the client's own behaviours are holding back the business: for example, where a shy and introverted business owner was reluctant to go out and make new sales. We help the client find ways of overcoming these barriers: for example, by identifying circumstances where the client has successfully done so in the past.

Key issues

The coaching intervention follows the standard coaching pattern of regular one-hour or one-and-a-half hour meetings. However, the intervals between meetings, 2–3 months, are much longer than is normal for coaching. This is to give clients enough time to make changes in their business and see the results before the next coaching session.

The coaching context provides a supportive environment that allows the client to explore aspects of their business and personal situation that might provoke anxiety and enables the anxiety to be contained. This containment also helps the client to think creatively.

As indicated above, we use Appreciative Inquiry techniques. Appreciative Inquiry has been described as "the art and practice of asking questions that strengthen a system's capacity to apprehend, anticipate and heighten positive potential" (Cooperrider & Whitney, 1999). Cooperrider and Whitney emphasize the central importance of affirmative topic choice: asking questions that focus on the positive aspects of a topic, rather than on identifying problems. Difficulties encountered by the client are addressed, but through clarifying the objective the client would like to attain and identifying examples of successful behaviour that the client can build on. We felt that the emphasis on the positive that is characteristic of Appreciative Inquiry fitted well with the psychological characteristics typical of small business leaders, for example, achievement orientation and internal locus of control, and this has proved to be the case in practice.

In the appreciative questions and reflective process, we also encourage clients to consider their leadership qualities. This is particularly important for clients thinking of setting up their own business. The coaching team encourages the client to consider the qualities required to lead the proposed business and their own characteristics, and deduce their developmental needs. The relevant characteristics might include, for example, level of social functioning and network, ability to give work sufficient priority in relation to life and family needs, the degree to which their individual approach includes taking responsibility, how they could reframe setbacks and challenges, and personal drive to succeed.

To assess the client's work–life balance, we adopted a personal coaching model, "The Seven Domains of Life", that in our experience effectively categorizes the main aspects of an individual's life. The domains identified by the model are Finance, Health, Work, Personal Relationships, Family and Extended Family, Friends and Social Life, and Spirituality (Mulligan, 1999). This model identifies discrete domains of life in which clients can identify their goals; we use it as a checklist to ensure that the client has thought about what they expect in each of these domains.

We found that it is important to establish a profile of the client's work–life balance because often the commitment required to achieve the work goal is undermined by needs from the family and personal relationship domains. We observed that the clients who were more likely to succeed were those whose needs were not focused on short-term financial gain or personal income to improve life style, but on a genuine interest in developing the project or business idea. Such clients are more likely to integrate their goals in the various Domains of Life in such a way that they support, or at least do not undermine, their business.

Drawing on both coaching and consultancy techniques, we are able to place more emphasis on the consultancy or coaching aspects of our approach, depending on the client's needs. The choice of style depends upon whether the business is already established and the extent to which innovation or implementation of new business systems is required.

Method 2: Business and marketing consultancy for high-tech start-ups

Context

The Scottish Executive implemented two schemes, SMART and SPUR (now SMART: SCOTLAND), to help SMEs develop new commercially feasible products and processes involving a significant technological advance. Evaluations of the impact of these programmes and subsequent research by the Scottish Executive Enterprise, Transport & Lifelong Learning Department showed that SMART and SPUR beneficiaries could improve their business performance by researching their markets more carefully prior to launch. The Department therefore introduced an additional marketing and business support element for SMART and SPUR award winners: they were offered market analysis to clarify market requirements, and a business review based on a SWOT analysis to identify other critical factors facing the business.

Following a competitive tender exercise, Network Strategies Ltd (NSL) was one of several companies awarded a framework contract to provide the marketing and business support, and NSL was subsequently commissioned to consult to some of the award-winning SMEs. The first-named author was a member of the team that developed the methodology and delivered the consultancy.

Some of the SMEs we worked with had not yet launched their first product; others had an established business but were introducing a new product. They ranged in size from two to twenty employees.

Our approach

Business review

To carry out a business review based on a SWOT analysis, we initially set up a review framework identifying the major areas in which strengths and weaknesses would need to be assessed, taking account of the nature of the company. Typically, they would be the main areas of focus for business planning. For a company manufacturing bespoke products they might be:

- sales;
- marketing;
- customer support;
- engineering;
- manufacturing;
- management, resources, and finance.

Within each of these areas we provisionally identified a number of sub-areas to guide our information collection.

We started our work with each business with a structured workshop with the directors, to provide a thorough overview of the business and identify important information sources and people to interview. The workshop typically took half a day.

We then identified and reviewed key documents, e.g., business plans, and carried out individual interviews with directors and senior managers. The interviews provided information about company strengths and weaknesses, but also gave us an opportunity to assess the skills, experience, and alignment with company objectives of the individuals concerned.

To complete our review, we contacted one or two people outside the company, for example, a customer, contractor or distributor, to check whether external perceptions of the company were in accord with the internal view. We then drafted our initial findings and reviewed them in a workshop with the directors of the client company. Often, these workshops generated new information and raised important questions, which required us to undertake further information gathering, revise our findings, and discuss them again with the directors. When we arrived at a stable view of the company's strengths, weaknesses, and market position, we documented our findings and recommendations in a report.

Typically, a team of two consultants carried out the review; this allowed consultants with complementary areas of expertise to contribute, and, in our experience, the interaction between the team members led to more balanced judgements and a better quality review.

Market analysis

As part of the business review, we assessed the market information collected by the client company, and identified the nature and extent of requirements for additional market information. In particular, we reviewed the quality of the available information on:

- market characteristics, mapping, and segmentation;
- market size and growth forecasts;
- target customers, their needs and profiles;
- for business markets, the purchasing decision process, participants, and their roles;
- routes to market and the roles and requirements of participants in the distribution chain;
- competing products, their features, pricing, promotion, and distribution;
- competitor organizations, their positioning, strengths and weaknesses, and the intensity of competition.

As a first step to filling any gaps in the market information available, we reviewed market data published online and in paper-based media. We also contacted one or two people to check the quality of the available information, for example, an end user, a contractor, a distributor, or a market expert. Where these sources did not provide adequate information, we had the option of carrying out primary market research.

Key issues

SWOT analysis is a standard management and consultancy tool (for example, see McDonald, 1999). The key to success in these projects was to ensure that the framework for the analysis appropriately reflected important business functions. For the high-tech start-up businesses concerned there was a risk of weaknesses in sales and marketing; we were, therefore, particularly concerned that sales, marketing, and customer service functions were appropriately covered. We developed the review framework for each business on the basis of our experience and our discussions with the management.

The consultancy approach corresponded to the classic data analysis and feedback method: data collected by the consultants were fed back to the company managers at a review meeting (Block, 2000). However, carrying out these review meetings successfully was a test of our client management skills. The owner–managers were typically highly motivated people risking their careers to pursue a vision. Some of them had incurred significant start-up costs and ongoing costs for staff salaries and premises, but had not yet developed a revenue stream; it was potentially an anxious time. Initially, we encountered a degree of defensiveness, and also apparent unwillingness to prioritize the work, although the managers concerned had requested the review. The fact that our review had been commissioned through their funding agency undoubtedly contributed to their disquiet.

To minimize these difficulties, it was particularly important that our approach was friendly and supportive; we went out of our way to work closely with the clients and involve them in the research and analysis process. This helped them to overcome their anxieties about the review and understand our way of working, and enabled them to accept our questioning as constructive and open up to discuss any issues they faced. As a result, we were able to complete the reviews successfully and help some clients address potentially difficult issues.

Method 3: Information technology (IT) consultancy for small and medium-sized enterprises in a rural area

Context

Lincolnshire County Council (LCC), a local authority in England, commissioned a project to provide information and communications technology (ICT) consultancy to up to 500 SMEs in its area. The area is rural and relatively remote from major centres of population.

The project was part of a programme, the Lincolnshire Broadband Initiative, whose objective was to promote economic development and employment in the area by stimulating demand for broadband Internet services and the use of ICT applications within businesses.[2] The consultancy was intended to address a perceived shortfall among SMEs in the area in the skills required to exploit ICT. Grant funding was available to help businesses implement the ICT applications identified in the consultancy. The project was jointly funded by LCC and the European Regional Development Fund (ERDF).

Following a competitive tender exercise, Mantix Ltd, a project and programme management company, was selected as lead contractor to deliver the ICT consultancy. Mantix (now Atkins Management Consultants) assembled and managed a team of independent consultants to provide advice to the individual SMEs. The first-named author was a member of the team that worked with LCC to develop the methodology and delivered the consultancy.

Businesses wishing to apply for the consultancy completed and submitted an online form to Lincolnshire Broadband Initiative, using a sophisticated website designed for the purpose. The form requested some basic information about the business. Applications were screened by LCC staff to ensure their eligibility. Details of businesses eligible to receive the consultancy and the information they provided were passed to Mantix.

Our approach

The consultancy approach developed for the project had to meet a number of criteria.

- It had to work effectively for the businesses concerned, and deliver recommendations that they would subsequently implement.
- It had to be sufficiently clearly defined to be carried out by a team of about a dozen consultants, the number necessary to advise 500 businesses over the two-year timescale of the project.
- It had to make efficient use of consultants' time, so that consultancy could be provided to a large number of businesses within a set budget.

- It had to be auditable by the funding bodies, the local authority and the European Commission.

Our approach had a number of clearly defined stages.

1. When Mantix received details of a business eligible to receive consultancy, a consultant was assigned to the business and given the information submitted by it.
2. The consultant telephoned the business and had an initial conversation with the key manager about the business, its current ICT systems, and the issues it faced.
3. The business completed a detailed questionnaire about its business and ICT systems, and what it wanted out of the ICT consultancy.
4. The consultant had a meeting with the key business manager(s) at which the issues faced by the business, its plans for growth, and how ICT systems might support them were discussed in detail.
5. The consultant prepared a draft report reviewing the situation of the business and recommending ICT systems to help it achieve its objectives.
6. The consultant reviewed the draft report with the key managers in a second meeting.
7. The consultant revised the report in the light of the discussion and submitted a final version.

In the initial telephone contact, the consultant identified the most appropriate manager or managers to be involved in the consultation. The individuals concerned needed between them to be familiar with the future plans of the business and the issues it faced, and also with its ICT systems. For the smaller businesses, this was typically the managing director, whereas in larger businesses the managing director was often accompanied by the director whose responsibilities included ICT. In the largest businesses involved in the project, medium-sized companies of up to 250 employees, the point of contact was often an IT director or manager. During the course of the initial telephone conversation, the consultant briefed the manager concerned on the process to be followed, and the business was subsequently sent the questionnaire and a description of the consultancy process.

The responses to the questionnaire gave the consultant a good understanding of the commercial and IT situation of the business, and enabled him/her to prepare for the meeting with the business. The responses identified the issues the business wanted to address, and also provided enough information for the consultant to identify, on the basis of their experience, other issues that the business might need to address.

The first face-to-face meeting with the business was an opportunity to explore in detail its aspirations, and the commercial and IT issues it faced. Although the initial telephone call and questionnaire gave the consultant a checklist of topics to cover, the meeting was conducted as an open-ended conversation, and the consultant had to respond to and explore any issue that came up. It was therefore very important that the consultant could establish a rapport with the manager, and give an informed response to any issue that arose. However, although tentative solutions could be discussed, it was not necessary for the consultant to produce definitive answers at the first meeting. These meetings lasted between one and four hours, depending on the complexity of the business, the number of ICT issues to be discussed, and the personal styles of the participants.

Over a two- to three-week period, the consultant then prepared a detailed report analysing the business situation of the business, and recommending actions relating to ICT systems that would help the business to achieve its objectives and reduce ICT-related risks. In some cases, consultants made telephone contacts with the business during this period to check points of detail. Recommendations for ICT solutions were presented in a specification format where possible, rather than as a named product. (This format helped businesses to obtain competitive quotations from the market in support of their subsequent applications for project grant funding and present an effective "best value" assessment as part of their application.) The draft report was then e-mailed to the business, and the second meeting scheduled when the relevant managers had had a chance to review the report.

The second meeting provided the business managers with an opportunity to correct any inaccuracies in the report relating to the current situation of the business and its future plans. It also provided them with an opportunity to talk through the recommendations relating to ICT systems, to understand fully what was involved, and the implications for their business. The consultant could then correct any factual inaccuracies and fine-tune the recommendations for the business before submitting the final version of the report.

Key issues

The consultancy approach was again based on data analysis and feedback. However, the specifics of the approach enabled relevant data to be gathered in a very efficient manner. The issues to be addressed start to be identified in the first telephone conversation, and asking the client to fill in a relatively detailed questionnaire before the first meeting provides the consultant with a substantial base of data that can be used to prepare appropriate lines of questioning for the first meeting. Submitting a draft report and reviewing it at the second, feedback meeting enables the consultant's understanding of the situation to be tested out, so that any misunderstandings can be identified and eliminated before the final recommendations are delivered. The second meeting also provides a forum for the manager to discuss the feedback provided in the report, stimulating the manager to engage with the content and increasing his or her motivation to introduce change (Block, 2000). In the small business context, it is essential for the manager to take ownership of a change for it to happen.

The idea of identifying the technology and working arrangements required to support planned business developments can be traced back to socio-technical systems thinking (Trist & Murray, 1993). However, there is relatively little flexibility to accommodate different working arrangements in the ICT systems available to small businesses. It is almost always more cost effective to buy packaged software products than have bespoke software developed for a particular business. The cost of developing packaged software is spread over substantial numbers of purchasers, so that the software offers more features and is usually more reliable and has a better user interface than bespoke developments. There is often little scope for adapting packaged software to the working patterns of a particular business, so that the business has to adjust its processes to use the software. Websites are an exception, since they can usually be designed to the specific requirements of the business.

The strong sense of self-belief of many small business founders does not make them natural clients for consultancy advice, and many would be deterred from hiring consultants by concerns over the potential cost. However, the external funding of the consultancy and the prospect of access to grant funding for upgrading their ICT systems led to excellent take-up of the consultancy, with the full quota allowed by the funding being taken up. We believe that in almost all cases the business case for the recommended ICT improvements identified benefits far in excess of the actual cost of the consultancy.

To be successful, the consultants needed to establish a rapport with the small business managers. The process for selecting consultants for this work was designed to maximize the chances of success. All the consultants chosen were experienced, and ran their own independent consultancy businesses; they were, therefore, small business managers in their own right, and well placed to understand the issues of the small businesses to which they were consulting. Many of the small business managers commented at the end of the consultation how much they had valued the opportunity to discuss their business on a peer-to-peer basis with someone outside the business who understood the issues; they had few opportunities to do so. The knowledge of the small business environment that the consultants brought appears to have made a substantial contribution to their success. However, their consultancy skills to engage with the client and make them feel sufficiently at ease to share sensitive information about their business were equally important.

Conclusions

We have found the three consultancy approaches described above to be applicable with a wide range of small businesses. They deal with issues common to many small businesses and take account of the distinctive characteristics of small businesses and their managers. Each benefits to a greater or lesser extent from a mindfulness approach to work effectively with small business managers.

1. Our coaching for people considering setting up a small business is rooted in a mindfulness approach. Both of us have had relevant training, and our theoretical framework is informed by the psychology of mindfulness.
2. In our business and marketing consultancy for high-tech start-ups, we needed to work sensitively with the anxieties of the business managers around the review process. Handling these anxieties appropriately was essential to complete the reviews.
3. A mindfulness approach was not essential to carry out the IT consultancy. However, consultancy skills to engage with the clients and put them at ease were important, and the consultancy was valued for meeting psychological as well as technical needs, in providing an opportunity for small business managers to discuss their business on a peer-to-peer basis.

The ability to listen and empathize without preconceptions or projections, the essence of a mindfulness approach, is of great value in all consultancy work with small businesses.

Acknowledgements

The author is grateful to the Scottish Government and Network Strategies Ltd for permission to publish Method 2. The Mantix team who worked with Lincolnshire County Council to develop Method 3 and delivered the consultancy was led by Jim Blakelock and Kevin Sefton. The author is grateful to Lincolnshire County Council and Atkins Management Consultants for permission to publish this description.

Notes

1. This paper is a contribution to the Tavistock Institute programme "Refreshing The Tavistock Institute's Intellectual Traditions".
2. The original aim of the Lincolnshire Broadband Initiative was to provide consultations for 400 SoHo/micro businesses (1–9 employees) and 100 small/medium businesses (10–249 employees), reflecting the relative percentages of SMEs of these sizes in the project area. A fixed

price contract was negotiated on this basis, with different values assigned to consultations with businesses of different sizes. In practice, there was more demand for consultancy from small/medium businesses, so that the actual numbers delivered within the agreed fixed price ceiling were 352 SoHo/micro and 132 small/medium, a total of 484 businesses. The European Regional Development Fund (ERDF) target for the funding was 420 in total, so both scenarios exceeded this.

References

Block, P. (2000). *Flawless Consulting*. San Francisco, CA: Pfeiffer.

Bridge, S., O'Neill, K., & Cromie, S. (2003). *Understanding Enterprise, Entrepreneurship and Small Business*. Basingstoke: Palgrave Macmillan.

Cooperrider, D. L., & Whitney, D. (1999). A positive revolution in change: appreciative inquiry. In: P. Holman & T. Devane (Eds.), *The Change Handbook* (pp. 245–262). San Francisco, CA: Berrett-Koehler.

Cooperrider, D. L., Whitney, D., & Stavros, M. (2005). *Appreciative Inquiry Handbook*. San Francisco, CA: Berrett Koehler.

Department for Business, Enterprise and Regulatory Reform (2007). *Statistical Press Release URN 07/92*, 22 August. London: BERR.

Furnham, A. (1992). *Personality at Work*. London: Routledge.

GEM (2001). *Global Entrepreneurship Monitor 2001 UK Executive Report*. London: London Business School.

Germer, C. K. (2005). Mindfulness: What is it? What does it matter? In: C. K. Germer, R. D. Siegel, & P. R. Fulton (Eds.), *Mindfulness and Psychotherapy* (pp. 3–27). New York: Guilford.

Gumpert, D., & Boyd, D. (1984). The loneliness of the small-business owner. *Harvard Business Review, November–December*: 18–23.

Kets de Vries, M. (1977). The entrepreneurial personality: a person at the crossroads. *Journal of Management Studies, 14*: 34–57.

Kets de Vries, M. (1985). The dark side of entrepreneurship. *Harvard Business Review, November–December*: 160–167.

McDonald, M. (1999). *Marketing Plans*. Oxford: Butterworth Heinemann.

Morgan, G. (1986). *Images of Organization*. Beverly Hills, CA: Sage.

Mulligan, E. (1999). *Life Coaching: Change Your Life in 7 Days*. London: Judy Piatkus.

Storey, D. J. (1994). *Understanding the Small Business Sector*. London: Routledge.

Trist, E., & Murray, H. (1993). *The Social Engagement of Social Science: Vol. II—The Socio-Technical Systems Perspective.* Philadelphia, PA: University of Pennsylvania Press.

Turquet, P. (1974). Leadership: the individual and the group. In: G. S. Gibbard, J. J. Hartman, & R. D. Mann (Eds.), *Analysis of Groups: Contributions to Theory, Research, and Practice* (pp. 337–371). San Francisco, CA: Jossey-Bass.

CHAPTER SIX

When consultants collaborate and when they do not: some reflections on experience and practice

Maura Walsh and Sue Whittle

Introduction

This chapter turns the spotlight on the issues that can arise when consultants collaborate—and when they do not. It is written for those who consult in association with others, either as internal consultants to large organizations or as external consultants, practising independently or on an employed basis. Whether the consulting task is perceived as straightforward or more complex, many consulting collaborations fail, some never get off the ground, and others flounder at some point along the way. Many things can influence the outcomes of consulting interventions, but the chances of success are inevitably diminished if members of the consulting team will not or cannot work together productively.

From our experiences of working with other consultants, we wanted to address the following questions.

- Are some contexts (and some consultants) non-starters for collaborative consulting?
- What signs can indicate chances of survival and fruition and, conversely, chances of abortion and stagnation?

- Why do some collaborations take off and develop into creative and rewarding partnerships while others fail to get off the ground?
- What, if anything, can be done early in the life cycle of consulting collaborations (before the work is finally agreed, or contracted) to improve the chances of survival and success?

What supports and what gets in the way of consultants working together is clearly of interest to consultants and to their clients. In times of increasing consultancy specialisms (IT, change management, waste reduction, payment and reward systems, etc.), and with client demands to change everything at once (Neumann, Holti, & Standing, 1996), the consulting environment can be described as "turbulent" (Emery & Trist, 1965).

In turbulent environments, high levels of interdependence and complexity generate uncertainty—ideal conditions for stirring up anxieties and regressive behaviours. Yet there is very little published work on how consultants succeed in working together (or how and why they fail). The consequences of dysfunctional collaborations can be significant. In sectors such as the construction industry, urban regeneration, transport, prison services, broadcasting, and auditing, groups of consultants often come together as consortia, tasked with leading and evaluating sector level change strategies. Such consortia are highly formative, influencing the design and management of many organizations. Unresolved pressures, acted out in the consulting team, can lead consortia to play it safe or to project consultant issues on to clients as unwilling, unable, or unworthy. This can compromise change in the sector for years to come.

We focus on consulting practice and the activities and contexts shaping collaboration between practitioners. Our concern is with collaboration not as a noun (something that is, or something that we have) but as a verb (something that we do—or do not do). In drawing on the authors' experiences of working in both successful and unsuccessful collaborations with other consultants (including the writing of this chapter), we identify issues to bear in mind.

Literature

The literature is full of advice on how to design and manage networks, partnerships, and alliances (Bresnen & Marshall, 2000;

Swan, Newell, Scarbrough, & Hislop, 1999; Tracey & Clark, 2003). Research across a number of sectors and occupations reveals some consistency in the factors said to influence and shape collaboration; for example, a report by Vangen and Huxham (2003) provides a list of typical actions for improving collaboration, which should

- have clarity of purpose and objectives;
- deal with power differences;
- have leadership but do not allow anyone to take over;
- allow time to build up understanding;
- share workload fairly;
- resolve different levels of commitment;
- have equal ownership and no point scoring;
- accept that partnerships evolve over time.

In their own words, these "do not provide much in the way of pragmatic help" for intervening to support nascent and difficult collaborations (*ibid.*). Not much change from 1991, when *The Journal of Applied Behavioural Science* ran two special editions on collaboration in which editors Wood and Gray decried how some theories "leap from preconditions to outcomes, leaving us with a 'black box' to cover the area in between" (Wood & Gray 1991, p. 143). Given the propensity for consultants to work with others (Freedman & Zackrison, 2001), it is surprising that so little has been written that gets to grips with the complexities of collaborative consulting. Instead, the term "collaboration" is often used naïvely to describe how people work together on a time-bound project with little advice about how to achieve the types of prescriptions listed by Vangen and Huxham and others.

Papers by Empson (2001) and Beatty (2002) are recent exceptions. Beatty describes working with her father and how, by taking up different role relationships (based on information exchange, power differentials, and complementary skills), their collaboration endured. Getting stuck in any one role (the power dominated parent–child or student–teacher relationships, for example) would have inhibited the exchange of valuable information and access to the skills of both parties. In Beatty's experience, the choice of role relationship, consciously or compulsively, shapes the collaborative structures and determines who does what (Lawrence, 1999).

She points out that we tend to assume reciprocity in role relationships—that in defining her working relationship as child–parent, she assumes her father relates to her as parent to child. But this may not be the case, since relationships are dynamic, shifting with context and unconscious concerns. Tuning in to the variety of role relationships in play at any one time, and the clashes and collusions between them, offers a richer repertoire for collaboration and the opportunity to work with the less appropriate and regressive elements.

Empson (2001) looked at knowledge transfer in mergers in accounting and management consulting firms. She found that consultants resist using the knowledge of their newfound colleagues when they perceive that the merging firms differ fundamentally in terms of the quality of their external image and the forms of their knowledge bases. Individuals with a predominantly tacit knowledge base placed less value on the codified knowledge of their new colleagues. More surprising is the finding that individuals with the relatively codified knowledge base also placed little value on the tacit knowledge of their new colleagues. This emphasizes the extent to which the value and legitimacy of knowledge within organizations are shaped by highly subjective considerations (*ibid.*, p. 858).

It is our experience also that rational explanations barely skim the surface in terms of understanding what goes on and explaining why consultants find collaboration a challenge. This is all the more surprising in that many consultants are advising their clients on this very matter.

Literature that draws on psychodynamic perspectives, exploring subjectivity, anxiety, and identity issues, offers different insights. Zagier Roberts (1994) draws attention to the relationship between choice of profession, individual internal needs, and ego defences. She suggests that all professions have preferred working practices, mental models, and deep-rooted assumptions about the world that govern decision-making and behaviour (Argyris, 1985; Kuhn, 1972). In every profession, and especially in an emerging profession such as consultancy, competing paradigms and attachments to those paradigms (Bowlby, 1988; Klein, 1959) make collaborations problematic. As a result, collaborations frequently suffer from too much or too little "togetherness" as consultants huddle to ward off anxieties or divide up the work to avoid contact. The challenge for consultants is to find ways to bring to the surface and manage their default modes, those unconscious reactions that emerge when they are under pressure of one sort or another (Bowlby, 1988), in ways that do not trigger defensive behaviours, such as irritation, boredom, or attention seeking, in their colleagues.

Methodology

As a step to theory building (Eisenhardt, 1989), generalizing from experience depends on adequate definition of concepts. Looking across the literature on collaboration, we find we are in step with Nathan and Mitroff (1991) who describe collaboration in terms of "a group of key stakeholders [who] work together to make joint decisions about the future of their problem domain" (p. 169).

Their concept of negotiated order we have found speaks to our experiences and fits well with Gray's definition of collaboration as "a process through which parties who see different aspects of a problem can constructively explore their differences and search for solutions that go beyond their own limited vision of what is possible" (Gray, 1989, p. 5).

We have found this definition especially insightful in suggesting (1) that collaboration is a process rather than an outcome; (2) that the process of collaboration is only invoked when differences are perceived among those involved. Further, we agree with Wood and Gray that autonomy, although missing from much of the work on collaboration, is essential to understanding how collaborative relationships thrive and fail:

> ... for stakeholders retain their independent decision-making powers even when they agree to abide by shared rules ... if participants relinquish all autonomy, a different organizational form is created—perhaps a merger, but not a collaboration. [1991, p. 146]

Starting with experiences, we adopted an inductive approach (Gill & Johnson, 1991) to the development of our thinking, coupled with shared reflections on our here-and-now activity of writing this paper. Our experiences draw on multiple case examples (Mitchell, 1983) of consultant collaborations across assignments of varying lengths, with different sizes of consulting teams, in a range of sectors and intervention scenarios, as summarized in Table 1.

Reflecting on these cases, we identified their key characteristics and ran a comparative analysis moving between the data and literature sources. We found a great deal in common and much to think about in terms of what helps and hinders consultants to collaborate with others. By holding in mind the reader (a consulting practitioner audience) and frequently revisiting our understanding of the task, we have worked to resolve issues about what to leave in and what to leave out of our chapter.

Experiences of consulting collaborations and some propositions

The following vignettes describe four of the authors' collaborative consulting experiences and offer some observations and propositions.

Table 1.   Types of consultant collaborations.

Types of consulting work involving consultant collaborations	Group development workshops, residential conferences, work restructuring, evaluations, service redesigns, action research, policy implementation, inter-group dynamics
Sectors	Financial services, education, local government, construction, health services, voluntary sector, prison service, manufacturing
Number of consultants involved in each experience	2–11
Examples of professional identities of consultants involved	Organization development consultant, academic researcher, leadership couch, health economist, barrister, criminologist, accountant, business process consultant, procurement specialist, internal change manager
Length of assignment	3 months–4 years

Experience 1

An independent business process consultant, who had a large contract with a major financial organization to deliver a process improvement programme, invited me to design and deliver a workshop for project leaders on leading teams through projects. I noticed early on that the invitation to work on a "partnership basis" seemed to contradict my experience of being in a sub-contracted role (for example, he talked, I listened, but there was no real dialogue; he got irritated and impatient if I tried to engage in conversation about the intervention; he was happy for me to meet his client to plan the work, without him). After some reflection, I decided to try to put these concerns aside and "get on with the job".

I delivered the first workshop and got strong positive feedback from the client. Meanwhile, the consultant had told me that I had now joined his consulting team! This came as quite a surprise to me as we had not discussed it or contracted for it. The consultant was indignant at my reaction and terminated my contract shortly after.

Observations

● Insufficient time and apparent reluctance to invest in contracting over role and role relationships quickly caused problems—perhaps this was a non-starter?

● Different paradigms were operating on the resources, communication, and co-ordination required for successful outcomes; not surfaced sufficiently.

● His avoidant attachment style caused conflict: my requests for discussion were experienced as demanding; in turn, I adopted (defensive) self-reliance.

● No relationship was developed so no trust and little liking emerged.

● Request for discussion of contract may have been experienced as possible rejection (could not "swallow" it); I was rejected instead.

● Containing these emerging conflicts and anxieties until we were further on with the work might have given us a chance to develop a relationship, and therefore some trust, providing some firmer ground for such a conversation.

Experience 2

I needed to find a team to help me to develop a new intervention for the marketplace. I became aware of the conscious, and less conscious, factors that were influencing my choices: conscious factors included background, expertise, orientation, commonality, and diversity; less conscious factors were trust (whether I trusted them or not), liking (how much I liked them), and how I experienced them in terms of how they related to me and others (status, power, containment, attachment). I soon realized how much stronger the unconscious factors were.

Because this was a new venture, there was a high level of uncertainty and risk. Location meant that communication was largely by e-mail and phone with limited face-to-face contact. Different backgrounds (sectors and experience influencing working practices and norms) and orientations (for example, towards task; an up-front agreement *vs.* an emergent process) created differences and tensions that became valuable pivots in the discussions and were managed, if not always brought to the surface. In fact, openly addressing these regressive dynamics might have risked the assignment. The balance between the autonomy (of the individual) and the integration (of the intervention design) became critical when it began to have an impact on the task and outcome. Rather than addressing this on a personal basis, we addressed it on a client-centred and task basis. This was experienced as more rational and acceptable and perhaps "protected" the individual, and the team, from unnecessary personal scrutiny that might have hindered the work.

Observations

- There will always be differences to be managed even in apparently homogeneous teams.
- Managing regressive dynamics is not the same as openly addressing them
- Clashes and conflict arising from differences can be invigorating and developmental if consultants can (a) take a systems *vs.* an interpersonal perspective, and (b) provide containment to the individual and the group.
- Liking and trusting our colleagues in new ventures helps a great deal!

Experience 3

I was invited to work with a high profile consulting team on a fixed-term contract to deliver and develop interventions using experiential technologies. This offered an opportunity to collaborate with people I admired on the sort of work I knew would be challenging but developmental. I was flattered and anxious. Members of the team had established differentiated roles and responsibilities but I soon discovered that much of the control and co-ordination was managed through tacit routines and mutual adjustment within a non-negotiable structure to which they were strongly attached. My feelings were of being a stranger in a strange land, unsure of the rules. I was uncertain about whether asking for advice or help might be interpreted as incompetence and suggestions for change as impudence. The extent to which current working arrangements met consultant rather than client needs was clearly undiscussable, and yet anything approaching needy behaviour was frowned upon. An ethos of detached self-reliance was the preferred, but unspoken, *modus operandi,* as if the work was never a source of anxiety or alarm. This shaped relationships with clients, who were judged as "in need of development" if they desired proximity or reassurance from the consultants. Neither party sought to renew the collaboration at the end of the fixed term.

Observations

- Different consultants have learnt to manage their anxieties about their work and identities in different ways.
- Collaborating with others can bring these ways of dealing with alarm into conflict.
- Collaborating may threaten long-standing defensive structures to the point of making the collaboration impossible.
- The idea that structures offer defences against anxiety holds for consultants as well as clients.

Experience 4

A male consultant in his early thirties agreed to work with eight others, under the direction of an older woman (one of the authors), providing he could work with a part of the client system with which he had an established working relationship. He had good contacts and was respected for producing interesting ideas. Over the next few months, he failed to deliver the work as planned, "forgot" to share contact details, and attended, but did not participate in, consultant team meetings. He seemed to be following a different agenda. Of course, he was! Not long after, he started working for himself and expended a great deal of energy disparaging the work of the team and the work he had not done. Remaining colleagues were then involved in damage limitation with the client, rebuilding collaborative consulting relationships, and re-contracting. The experience continued to be a shadow through out the contract and severely affected resources.

Observations

- It may be naïve to assume that hierarchy and formal governance procedures can protect against exploitative behaviour.
- It is helpful to bear in mind that collaborating consultants will be at different stages in their professional and business development life cycles and might seize (unexpected) opportunities.
- In consulting, power is dispersed throughout the consulting group in relation to access to the client system. Relationships of trust, dependence, and influence between client and consultant can shift quickly and this can radically alter relations *between* consultants.

Reflections on experiences and some propositions

Through our analysis, we have identified the following taxonomy of collaborative consulting relationships: collaborating for resources; collaborating for innovation; collaborating for security; and collaborating cynically. We offer a number of propositions that relate to the issues arising in each of the scenarios.

Collaborating for resources

The resource-based view (Prahalad & Hamel, 1990) makes sense of collaboration as a rational activity designed to enhance the bundles of capabilities consultants have at their disposal. Here, collaboration between consultants is about accessing much needed resources (expertise, routes to market, reputation, technology) essential to achieving on-going consulting tasks (Gray, 1989; Gustafson & Cooper, 1978) and to developing consulting businesses.

Over time, intervention practices can become routine and repetitious as consultants concentrate on specific sectors, perhaps continue to work with the same few clients, or specialize in narrowly defined interventions or client problems. In these situations, consultants can be tempted to stretch their practice beyond their expertise and improvise inappropriately. "Making do" with the consultant resources at hand (Moorman & Miner, 1998) in heroic or narcissistic efforts to meet client needs is an indicator of a poorly developed sense of competence and/or integrity. In the resource-based view, collaboration can help to access clients in different ways by enabling consultants to tap into a wider range of practice domains and technical expertise without threatening their own professional competence. In so doing, collaboration from this perspective implies some acknowledgement, however implicit, of the limitations of the consultants' professional knowledge base.

Proposition 1: to collaborate for resources consultants need to be in touch with the boundaries of their competence and be able to reflect on the fit between the needs of their clients and their own expertise.

Proposition 2: to collaborate for resources consultants need to be mindful of the different approaches consultants bring to the entry and contracting stage of the consulting cycle (Neumann, 1997). In new collaborations, a "minimum critical specification" (Cherns, 1987) approach might allow the work to proceed successfully until the relationship has had a chance to develop to a more secure base.

Collaborating for innovation

Innovation is essential for the development of professional practice. The application of ideas generated in one sector to the issues faced by another sector is a well-worn innovation route. Collaborating with consultants with experiences of different sectors and/or with different intervention repertoires around a shared task of bringing something new to a specific market or client conjures up excitement and creativity that might lead to . . . who knows where? Crucially, consultants need to consider how much difference they can accommodate (Rogers, 1983) without compromising their craft.

Perhaps perversely, collaboration can also provide an idealized consulting environment where consultants flee from real world pressures and disappointments into a fantasy world of "what ifs". Potential regressive dynamics in this type of scenario include basic group phenomena (Bion, 1961) of (1) salvation and pairing, (2) relationships of rescue and dependence, or (3) collective fighting against a common external foe, such as current fashionable approaches, similar client irritations, and unfulfilling professional lives. In such scenarios, a rhetoric of collaborating for innovation can disguise the reality of collaborating for escape.

Proposition 3: the less reality testing of "new ideas" and proposals and the stronger the boundary put around consultants collaborating for innovation (evidenced, for example, by not revealing its existence to others), the more likely collaboration is meeting identity needs not met, or no longer met, elsewhere.

Collaborating for security

Consultants often prefer to work with others rather than work alone, to share ideas or to provide support when the going gets tough. Many groups of consultants differentiate roles and responsibilities (Menzies, 1960) and the advice that "it takes a group to consult to a group" is well known. While working with others can allow consultants to meet their dependency needs, side-step authority issues, and cope with identity anxieties, it is not always true that there is safety in numbers.

Task-based collaboration requires an adequate holding environment (Winnicott, 1965), but the development of such an environment might be prevented by inappropriate behaviours by group members. Here, consultants might experience themselves as abandoned by their colleagues or, alternatively, subject to excessive intrusion by members of the collaborating group (Balint, 1959; Gustafson & Cooper, 1978).

Uncertainty and the alarm it generates play a significant role in shaping collaboration in groups (Groves & Fisher, 2006). It is our experience that to sustain collaboration, consultants need to find ways to promote conditions of safety for those involved by being there when needed (rather than abandoning someone to their own devices), while at the same time not being overly intrusive and prescriptive. We have found that paying attention to attachment behaviours and indicators of attachment styles in our consulting collaborations is particularly helpful in crafting a secure base to provide containment in these inevitably strange situations (Bowlby, 1969).

Proposition 4: inappropriate behaviours can stir up feelings of abandonment and/or intrusion that hinder collaboration between consultants.

Proposition 5: awareness of one's preferred attachment style(s) and ability to diagnose the attachment styles of others helps consultants to manage the "strange situation" anxieties stirred up in collaborative relationships.

Bowlby identified a number of attachment styles, for example:

- Secure attachment: child is confident that parent/parent figure will be available, responsive, and helpful, especially in adverse/ frightening circumstances. Child develops confidence in their own ability to manage and survive alarming situations with the help of others.
- Anxious resistant attachment: child is uncertain whether parent/parent figure will be available, responsive, and helpful. Can become anxious about separation and anxious about exploring the world. Threats of abandonment may be used as means of control, producing internal conflict.
- Anxious avoidant attachment: child has no confidence in being responded to helpfully, indeed, expects to be rebuffed; becomes emotionally self-sufficient and may appear aloof.

Collaborating cynically

The message in much of the literature on collaboration is that working with others is advantageous. Many papers identify those issues that can hinder collaborative working, and Empson is no exception. She writes of how difficulties with knowledge transfer between consulting firms, while attributed to "commercial and objective concerns", can be impeded by "the twin fears of exploitation and contamination" (Empson, 2001, p. 839). Her paper discusses the resulting challenges to inter-firm collaboration if potential costs (e.g., managerial, emotional, and opportunity) and losses (including the firm's reputation and strategic position, and individual professional identities) have not been thought through. In our experience, too, consulting collaborations can offer opportunities for commercial espionage, for personal and professional sabotage, and opportunities to disparage the work of others.

It is not uncommon to hear of consultants who have had access to intervention designs and diagnostic techniques through a collaborative venture subsequently deploying these as if they were their own. This form of exploitation is almost taken for granted, so long as some cursory acknowledgement is given. We have also heard our materials being used by others as if these were *their* experiences. Somehow, this is experienced as more invasive. We find we have been involved in a number of relationships with other consultants where the collaboration is probably best described as "cynical". In one example, someone with no interest in the work presented themselves as enthusiastic to keep someone else out.

Proposition 6: the more instrumental is the relationship between consultants required to work collaboratively, the more likely that opportunities for exploitation will be acted upon.

Implications for collaborations

The world of collaboration

In analysing our experiences, we have identified nine elements in three zones that shape consulting collaborations. Together these comprise the world of collaboration—those visible and invisible forces that shape the environment in which consultant to consultant relationships thrive or perish. The model is shown in Figure 1, and presents three zones of consciousness that together interact to influence consultants' collaborations.

The *external world* of Zone 1 is the explicitly conscious zone where key elements shaping collaboration are:

- *roles*: both given to and taken up by those individuals involved in collaborative working;
- *tasks*: the work that each individual and the group of consultants is there to do;
- *governance*: how tasks and roles are organized, and by whom.

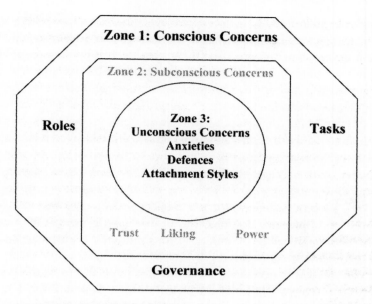

Figure 1.   The world of collaboration.

While this zone is the most consciously managed, clearly any one of these elements can be the subject of neglect and mindful forgetting.

In Zone 2, at the transitional, sub-conscious level, dominant shapers of collaboration are:

- *trust*: the extent to which individual consultants are honest with and have confidence in other individuals in the work group;
- *liking*: the pleasure or disdain stirred up by one individual for another;
- *power*: who is perceived as having influence over what, over whom, and in which contexts.

At the unconscious level lie those Zone 3 *inner world* elements of:

- *anxieties*: those feelings of unease, alarm, and terror that consultants learn to keep under control, most of the time;
- *defences*: those systems, processes, rituals and devices employed to protect us from our anxieties and escape from alarming situations;

● *attachment styles*: derived from early infant attachment to (m)other that influence how we relate to others. (See Bowlby for accessible reading on attachment styles and behaviours.)

Using the model

We have used this model to make sense of consulting collaborations both in the past and the "here and now". Clearly, these elements are interrelated, making collaborations complex and adaptive systems. One shift created in the system has an impact elsewhere: for example, a shift in one person's role (whether formal or informal) can have an impact on the task, the power distribution, and mutual liking, which will be experienced on some level by all members of the consulting team (see Beatty, 2002).

In using the model, we try to keep in mind differences between the three zones. These might be culturally specific. Zone 1 is the most "concrete", permitting anticipated discussion and negotiation; zone 2 may be considered less "concrete" and less valid as a legitimate item for conversation; zone 3 is possibly the least accessible and likely to evoke least appetite for explicit surfacing. In contracting for work, negotiations tend to address only four of the nine elements - "role", "task", and "governance" in zone 1, and "power" in zone 2. In our experience, *more than half of the elements that shape collaboration are unlikely to arise in a contracting conversation.*

Using the model can raise awareness of how the elements shape one's own and others' practices. It can serve to build dialogue to illuminate what is being attended to and what ignored by consultants who need to work together. This can help to create choices for consultants and consultant teams about whether and how to intervene to manage regressive dynamics. In this way, consultants can develop the capacity for keeping the "collaboration space" open, a vital mechanism for sustaining the well-being of the group and a task orientation. Whether the model is used "privately"—for back room reflections—or shared and processed with one's colleagues depends on the nature of the consulting relationship and the complexity and intensity of the dynamics. We have found that, however used, the model can be a powerful tool in processing, reframing, and making sense of consultant and consultant–client relationships.

We have found these ideas provide a helpful framework for thinking about what shapes collaboration and what needs to be managed when consultants try to work together. In the struggle to collaborate, consultants may attend to or neglect each and every zone, and difficulties can arise when any one zone dominates the leadership and management of the consulting team to the exclusion of others. Indeed, consultants may make the assumption that because they share similar or "mature" work practices, many of these influences will not affect them. We are convinced that all elements are present in all consulting collaborations. The extent to which they are present is likely to differ depending on macro (environmental, cultural) and micro factors (the type and mix of consultants, development of the consulting group over time, etc.). Different elements of the model are therefore likely to require greater attention in different circumstances and at different times. We aim to explore these issues further in subsequent work.

Conclusions

Collaboration is more than mere "working together". Collaboration means both ". . . working together on a project of common concern and benefit . . . [and] . . . to work along with opposition or enemies in betrayal of one's own class or kind" (Gustafson & Cooper, 1978, p. 156).

In our experience, this duality defines every collaborative relationship. The simultaneous presence of both senses of the word (working together and working in opposition) puts compromise at the heart of every act of collaboration. In "compromise", we refer to knowing (if perhaps not consciously acknowledging) that working with other consultants inevitably means:

1. Not following the consulting routines and behaviours that have worked well enough in the past.
2. Being willing to rethink or even dispense with some of those principles of consulting practice that define professional identity, thereby managing at times a sense of loss.
3. Having to cope with feelings of loss and anxiety when defensive structures and cherished transitional objects (such as

favourite tools and techniques) cannot be mobilized to provide comfort and containment in circumstances that generate alarm.
4. Looking for new ways to affirm a sense of self and professional worth.
5. Developing different strategies for using with different consulting groups, depending on their preferred orientations.

We have identified nine elements within three zones that shape the struggle to collaborate: role, task, governance, trust, liking, power, anxieties, attachment, and defensive structures. Issues within each element are never wholly resolved, but require constant attention over the life cycle of consulting collaborations.

In the early stages of an assignment, especially an innovative project where there may be no clear or agreed task defined, dysfunctional competitive relationships might emerge quickly in the struggle to collaborate (Freedman & Zackrison, 2001). This is evidenced by what is and what is not said; what is and is not shared; who leads and who follows; whose e-mails are answered and whose ignored; what gets attended to and what is left out; and whose ideas prevail. Differences in consultants' practice domains, (technical/psycho-social, or individual/group/organizational, for example) and their preferred paradigms (both epistemological and political) have some impact on how this is played out, as does each individual's attachment style (the main strategy each one of us has learnt in order to cope with situations that alarm us). Such differences are unlikely to be immediately apparent and therefore not available for negotiation or intervention until the collaboration is threatened. This can be signalled by: nothing happening; feelings of being left out or diminished in some way; resentment at "having to do all the work" or frustration about being overruled and discounted; feelings of jealousy and mistrust of others perceived to have a better relationship with colleagues or clients.

Further, we anticipate that the elements are interdependent, configuring (Miller, 1993) potential pathways for collaborative consulting work so that some seem to be "dead certs" and others "non-starters". But these summary judgements can be misleading, and we have described experiences in which our perhaps complacently cosy consulting relationship suddenly (and at the time inexplicably) turned.

All groups can work collaboratively and non-collaboratively and the challenge for consultants is how to work with regressive dynamics that get in the way of collaboration (Gustafson & Cooper, 1978). We hope our examples indicate that the decision to collaborate with other consultants is just the beginning. Working at collaboration in the here-and-now is a formidable challenge. For collaborations to survive, to endure and prosper, and to deliver developmental bene-fits rather than primarily meet regressive needs, those involved need access to ways of thinking about and intervening in the construction of collaborative relationships *in real time*.

The heuristics currently available to help such reflective practice fail to address the psychoanalytic forces that shape and threaten these relationships. Recognizing the need to attend to both task and relational processes is not new (Ancona & Caldwell, 1998; Hare, Borgatta, & Bales, 1965; Jehn, 1995; Stogdill & Coons, 1957). Reminding consultants of the relevance of these dynamics to their own practices, particularly in the temporary and ill-bounded contexts we have described, is novel.

We hope this initial taxonomy drawn from our own experiences of successful and failed collaborations and the collaboration zone model go some way towards helping consultants make sense of and intervene in working relationships to support professional and business development. To manage collaboration with clients, consultants need to manage collaboration with each other.

References

Argyris, C. (1985). *Strategy, Change & Defensive Routine*. Boston, MA: Pitman.

Ancona, D., & Caldwell, D. (1998). Rethinking team composition from the outside. In: M. A. Neale, E. A. Mannix, & D. H. Gruenfeld (Eds.), *Research on Managing in Groups and Teams* (Volume 1: *Composition*) (pp. 21–38). Greenwich, CT: JAI Press.

Balint, M. (1959). *Thrills and Regressions*. New York: International Universities Press.

Beatty, J. (2002). Me, Jack, and "The Head": collaborative frames at the Academy of Management. *Journal of Management Inquiry, 11*(3): 305–315.

Bion, W. (1961). *Experiences in Groups and Other Papers.* London: Tavistock.

Bowlby, J. (1969). *Attachment and Loss, Vol. 1: Attachment.* New York: Basic Books,

Bowlby, J. (1988). *A Secure Base: Parent–Child Attachment and Healthy Human Development.* New York: Basic Books,

Bresnen, M. J., & Marshall, N. (2000). Motivation, commitment and the use of incentives in partnerships and alliances. *Construction Management and Economics, 18*(5): 587–598.

Cherns, A. B. (1987). The principles of socio-technical design revisited. *Human Relations, 40*: 153–162.

Eisenhardt, K. M. (1989). Building theories from case study research. *Academy of Management Review, 14*(4): 532–550.

Emery, F. E., & Trist, E. L. (1965). The causal texture of organizational environments. *Human Relations, 18*: 21–31.

Empson, L. (2001). Fear of exploitation and fear of contamination: impediments to knowledge transfer in mergers between professional service firms. *Human Relations, 54*(7): 839–862.

Freedman, A., & Zackrison, R. E. (2001). *Finding Your Way in the Consulting Jungle.* San Francisco, CA: Jossey-Bass/Pfeiffer.

Gill, J., & Johnson, P. (1991). *Research Methods for Managers.* London: Paul Chapman.

Gray, B. (1989). *Collaborating: Finding Common Ground for Multi Party Problems.* San Francisco, CA: Jossey-Bass

Groves, K., & Fisher, D. (2006). Doing collaboration: the process of constructing an educational community in an urban elementary school. *Ethnography and Education, 1*(1): 53–66.

Gustafson, J. P., & Cooper, L. (1978). Collaboration in small groups: theory and technique of the study of small group processes. *Human Relations, 31*(2): 155–171.

Hare, A. P., Borgatta, E. F., & Bales, R. F. (Eds.) (1965). *Small Groups: Studies in Social Interaction.* New York: Knopf.

Jehn, K. A. (1995). A multimethod examination of the benefits and detriments of intragroup conflict. *Administrative Science Quarterly, 40*: 256–258.

Klein, M. (1959). Our adult world and its roots in infancy. *Human Relations, 12*: 291–303.

Kuhn, T. S. (1972). *The Structure of Scientific Revolutions.* Chicago, IL: University of Chicago Press.

Lawrence, W. G. (1999). A concept for today; the management of oneself in role. In: W. G. Lawrence (Ed.), *Exploring Individual and Organizational Boundaries* (pp. 235–249). London: Karnac.

Menzies, I. (1960). A case study in the functioning of social systems as a defence against anxiety. *Human Relations, 13*: 95–121.

Miller, E. (1993). *From Dependency to Autonomy: Studies in Organisation and Change*. London: Free Association.

Mitchell, J. C. (1983). Case and situational analysis. *Sociological Review, 31*: 187–211.

Moorman, C., & Miner, A. (1998). Organizational improvisation and organizational memory. *Academy of Management Review, 23*(4): 698–723.

Nathan, M. L., & Mitroff, I. I. (1991). The use of negotiated order theory as a tool for the analysis and development of an interorganizational field. *Journal of Applied Behavioral Science, 27*(2): 163–180.

Neumann, J. (1997). Negotiating entry and contracting. In: J. Neumann, K. Kellner, & A. Dawson-Shepherd (Eds.), *Developing Organisational Consultancy* (pp. 7–31). London: Routledge.

Neumann, J., Holti, R., & Standing, H. (1996). *Change Everything at Once*. Didcot: Management Books.

Prahalad, C. K., & Hamel, G. (1990). The core competence of the corporation. *Harvard Business Review, May–June*: 79–91.

Rogers, E. M. (1983). *Diffusion of Innovation* (2nd edn). New York: Free Press.

Stogdill, R. M., & Coons, A. E. (1957). *Leader Behavior: Its Description and Measurement*. Columbus, OH: Ohio State University.

Swan, J. A., Newell, S. M., Scarbrough, H., & Hislop, D. (1999). Knowledge management and innovation: networks and networking. *Journal of Knowledge Management, 3*(4): 262–275.

Tracey, P., & Clark, G. L. (2003). Alliances, networks and competitive strategy: rethinking clusters of innovation. *Growth and Change, 23*: 1–16.

Vangen, S., & Huxham, C. (2003). Nurturing collaborative relations building trust in interorganizational collaboration. *Journal of Applied Behavioral Science, 39*(1): 5–31.

Wood, D., & Gray, B. (1991). Towards a comprehensive theory of collaboration. *Journal of Applied Behavioral Science, 27*(2): 139–162.

Winnicott, D. W. (1965). *The Maturational Process and the Facilitating Environment*. New York: International Universities Press.

Zagier Roberts, V. (1994). The self-assigned impossible task. In: O. Obholzer & V. Roberts (Eds.), *The Unconscious at Work: Individual and Organizational Stress in the Human Services* (Chapter 12, pp. 110–118). London: Brunner- Routledge.

CHAPTER SEVEN

Executive coaching as an organizational intervention: benefits and challenges of a team of coaches working with multiple executives in a client system

Maria J. Nardone, Nancy D. Johnson, and Lawrence A. Vitulano

Introduction

E xecutive coaching was originally seen as a perk for high performing CEOs or a fix for selected derailing of senior level executives (Fitzgerald, 2002; Kampa-Kokesch, & Anderson, 2001; Kiel, Rimmer, Williams, & Doyle, 1996; Kilburg, 1996). The ultimate goal in the minds of the employers is generally to benefit the organization as a whole. It is believed that benefiting the individual executive would eventually have an impact on the organization. In the case we will present, the company's goals for their executive coaching programme included increasing senior leadership, thereby addressing succession issues, as well as pressures from changing markets, which were requiring organizational shifts. With the larger organizational picture in mind, the company's mandate to the coaches was to focus on the individual executive's specific developmental needs. Boyatzis and colleagues (Boyatzis, Smith, & Blaize, 2006) have shown that "instrumental coaching", which focuses on goals that are not motivated by the coachee's own desire to develop, will not have the positive benefit that coaching with the coachee's developmental needs in mind has. "Compliance coaching", another form of "instrumental coaching", which has the goal of persuading the coachee to accept an assignment or transfer, or to "fit in" to the organization's needs without regard for the person's developmental needs, is not likely be beneficial or rewarding. Coaching engagements that are primarily focused on the company's goals without regard for the executive's developmental needs are never successful (*ibid.*). The focus of this programme was to provide an opportunity for growth and development for its Vice Presidents. The executive coaching programme for leadership development was one of the company's investments in the development of its senior executives and the future of the company.

Some companies have identified competences that they believe are critical for success in their industry. Their coaching programmes focus on developing those competences. The organization we are presenting did not have specific competences identified. The emotional and social competences identified by the research of Boyatzis, Goleman, and the Hay Group were the basis of the programme (Hay Group/McBer, 1999, Hay Group, 2002). In addition, most senior executives of this company had the competencies to fill the role of marketer, project manager, or technical expert. Even before the coaches arrived, the organization knew that it was not fruitful to coach a person to be proficient in all roles, but to help an individual know his strengths and maximize them. Actually, more often, the coaching goal was to encourage an executive to relinquish multiple roles in favour of one. As the company grew, it was clear that executives would be more effective if they focused on their strengths and directed their efforts at a single role rather than trying to be successful at multiple roles.

A team model for executive coaches

Working together as a team of coaches is a critical aspect of our approach. Organizations may have several coaches working in their organization, but they do not necessarily work as a team, sharing organizational knowledge, providing peer supervision, and a forum for reflecting upon and evaluating the progression of the project. Working alone as a coach in an organization can be daunting. It is more difficult to resist the pulls into organizational politics and dynamics when working alone. A team can offer support, collaboration, and validation. Together, the team members can be mindful of maintaining roles and boundaries. There is opportunity for supervision from peers who also have first-hand knowledge and experience of the organization. We see the team approach as critical for the efficacy of our work. Working together provided us with an opportunity for discussion and debate among ourselves. In our meetings, we shared our observations, hypotheses, and approaches. As a result, our formulations were better developed than they would have been if we were working alone. Because we had consensus and peer validation, we believe we were more confident and effective in our interventions than we would have been working solo. It would not have been possible to accomplish alone what we were able to provide as a team of coaches working together.

Our model for executive coaching also reflects the approach of the Tavistock Institute's Advance Organization Consultation Programme, which is to bring knowledge and experience in three areas (organizational theory, psychodynamics, and consultancy practice) to each case. The authors are a team of psychologists from clinical, consulting, psychoanalytic, and organizational backgrounds. In addition, each of us had experience in business, including family businesses. Our multi-faceted background of psychology, organizational knowledge, and business experience provides a complex lens with which to view the client and organization, offering an advantage over coaches from a single background or experience. Psychologists working as coaches have several advantages (Winum, 2003). Psychologists are knowledgeable about a wide body of literature, including cognition, motivation, learning, social psychology, group dynamics, developmental psychology, neuropsychology, clinical, psychoanalytic, and industrial/organizational psychology, which is relevant for executive and organizational change. For example, cognition, motivation, and learning are relevant for understanding the change process. Social psychology and group dynamics are important for understanding how organizations work. Developmental, clinical, and psychoanalytic psychology, and neuropsychology are helpful in identifying issues that are beyond coaching and better addressed in other modalities, such as psychotherapy. Consider how frequently "time management" or "poor organizational skills" are a focus of concern. Both can be rooted in an attention deficit disorder, which psychologists are trained to identify. During our graduate work in psychology, we had extensive training in intellectual and personality assessment and feedback, which is critical for every coaching engagement. In addition, we have been certified in a number of multi-rater feedback tools, including the Emotional Competence Inventory (Hay/McBer, 1999; Hay Group, 2002), as well as natural ability assessments, such as the Highlands Ability Battery (Highlands, 2004) which we use regularly in our coaching assignments. Every coaching assignment begins with assessment, since identifying strengths and areas for development is crucial. Understanding what makes one successful and what is valued by others is often taken for granted. Focusing on developing strengths bears more rewards than dwelling on one's limitations (Boyatzis & McKee, 2005).

Coaching executives for leadership development facilitates increased self-awareness and behavioural change (Boyatzis & McKee, 2005; Goleman, 1998; Goleman, Boyatzis, & McKee, 2002). Psychologists understand principles of learning, motivation, and development, the foundation for successful behavioural change. We understand patterns of behaviour, including how ingrained and resistant to change they can be. Also, coaching is not therapy, and, with our clinical backgrounds, we know how to make the distinction and refer an executive for a psychiatric or psychological consultation when indicated. Sometimes depression or other psychological problems are misread as "laziness", "poor teamwork", or "unco-operativeness". Psychologists are experts in understanding human behaviour and relationships and therefore well suited to address the goals of leadership development, including improved self-awareness and effectiveness.

An executive coach who comes from a single background, such as a former business executive, would be at a disadvantage in coaching without a foundation in psychological principles. So, too, would we, if we did not have business experience and a knowledge of organizational theory and group dynamics. In our opinion, coaches who have a multi-faceted background, including psychological, organizational, and business experience, have a distinct advantage.

Our approach: a case study

The authors worked together as a team providing executive coaching for an organizational leadership development programme. Our coachees were Vice Presidents of an international consulting firm. Our coaching assignments for each officer lasted approximately one year. The programme began with a four-day retreat led by the top executive team (CEO, President, and CFO) and the organizational development leader from HR. The retreat, which included team building exercises and discussions about leadership, was the formal opening of the executive coaching programne. After the retreat, the President of the company met with the coaches to debrief us about the retreat, which included some description of the group dynamics and characteristics of the current class of executives as well as a synopsis of each coachee, including his or her current role and the company's hopes and expectations for him or her. In our experience, support and endorsement from the top leadership is critical to a programme's success. It serves as motivation for a new coachee and can be helpful in minimizing resistance to an unfamiliar and anxiety-provoking process. This programme had endorsement from top leadership. The President and CEO had coaching, and not only endorsed the programme, but set an example for others to follow.

The coaches met as a team once per quarter to review our individual work and to discuss organizational issues. We found peer support and feedback critical in working with more than one executive over time in a large organization. Sharing our work, we were able to provide peer supervision for each other. If working alone, it is very difficult for the coach to be ever mindful of the potential pulls that can get one entangled in company politics and dynamics. Listening to each other's work, we could alert each other to potential problems, which might not have been recognized without a peer group as a sounding board. For example, there were occasionally attractive offers to do work for a coachee's client, which were enticing, but would have compromised the coaching relationship. If we were providing a service to our coachee's client, we would have been working with him for his client, and would thus become a peer. Or, if we were doing work he should be doing himself, we would become, in Peter Block's terms, "a pair of hands", rather than coach and consultant (Block, 1981). Our coaches' meetings were forums for airing these dilemmas. The meetings were an opportunity to present challenges and hear ideas from others that might be beneficial. Pooling and sharing organizational knowledge benefited both us and our client. In sharing our impressions, we gave each other confirmation and validation. Sometimes, our different perspectives were also enlightening. Together we would end up with a broader and richer view of an issue than we would have alone. Our meetings were invaluable to our work.

As with any working group, there were differences in style and opinion among the coaches. There were also issues of competition, such as who might be getting more work or the more desirable coaching assignments. We were always able to work through these issues. Upon reflection, we noted that we had the five conditions that Hackman (2002) has shown are essential for an effective high performing team: that is, we were a real team, we had an enabling structure, a compelling direction, a supportive organizational context, and expert coaching. We were not only coaching our clients, we were coaching each other. Hackman and Wegman (2007) also list three criteria essential for team effectiveness: positive task output, increasing competence of team members, and team experiences fostering the growth and well-being of its members. Our coaching team was producing an output that was valued by those who received it. Feedback about our work from our coaches and management was positive. Over time, we became increasingly competent in working together as a team. Our personal growth and well-being was fostered by our team experiences. For example, we presented our work at professional workshops and we took continuing education seminars together. Working together as a team was an essential ingredient for our work satisfaction.

In addition to team structure, and essential criteria for effectiveness, Hackman and his colleagues identify three essential process elements that are the core for successful teams. They are positive effort, effective strategy, and knowledge sharing and skill learning (Hackman, 2002; Hackman & Wegman, 2007). Positive effort is defined by Hackman and Wegman as a "high shared commitment to our work together and the team". Our work together was stimulating and rewarding. We looked forward to our client and team meetings. For the second element, effective strategy, we developed a work strategy that was uniquely appropriate to our task and situation and that we found highly effective. We developed a structure and process for our quarterly coaches' meetings that was efficient and effective. Each meeting included a review of our individual work, an update from the company's HR representative, and discussion about organizational issues and challenges facing the company. Finally, to Hackman's third point, "knowledge sharing and skill learning", our quarterly meetings helped to develop our knowledge and skill. We came to this project as independent consultants. We did not know each other before this assignment. Our common link was that each of us knew the company representative who hired us. In the course of our work together, we forged an effective team. We brought different perspectives from our varied experiences. No one person dominated the group. We listened and learned from each other. Over time, we developed an effective model for working as a team, coaching each other, as we provided executive coaching for this organization.

In our quarterly meetings, we also had input from the HR manager, who was the executive coaching programme manager. He was our client contact, who provided us with organizational updates and further information on the culture and climate of the company. During our tenure, we also met on occasion with an external organizational consultant, who was hired to help design and manage the company's reorganization of its business units. All too often, companies engage in a multiple change process with little communication among the leaders of the various efforts. In our experience, communication and sharing of organizational information among consultants is beneficial for the organization and the consultants. We had the benefit of support from top management. We also had communication from top management, our internal client representative, and external consultants, who were also working with the company. We consider all of these factors critical to the success of our work.

The frequency of contact with our coachees varied, depending on the individual's needs and the distance travelled. For example, if a coach was travelling across the country for a coaching session, he or she might spend all day with the client and frequency of face-to-face meetings might be once per month, whereas if the coach and client were local, they might have shorter, but more frequent meetings. Each coaching assignment began with an assessment that included interviews with the coachee, co-workers, supervisors, direct reports, and usually a family member, conducted by the coach. Including a family member, usually a spouse, in the process, was particularly helpful to provide information about work–life balance. In addition, the Emotional Competency Inventory (Hay/ McBer, 1999; Hay Group, 2002), an online multi-rater assessment tool, was administered. The assessment was followed by comprehensive feedback, after which individual coaching goals were developed and operationalized with specific action plans and measurement criteria. We recommended a minimum of six months of coaching for sustainable growth and change. We have compiled a list of coaching goals from our work that serve to illustrate the focus of our coaching interventions (Table 1). Since we regularly use the Emotional Competence Inventory in our work, many of the developmental goals are derived from Hay's list of competences, which distinguish outstanding from average leaders. Also, as other practitioners have already stated, it is important to emphasize maximizing strengths rather than focusing on weaknesses (e.g., Boyatzis & McKee, 2005).

Table 1. Developmental goals.

1. Increase emotional self-awareness
2. Increase self-confidence
3. Improve internal communication skills (schedule regular staff meetings, publish monthly update memo, etc.)
4. Improve organizational skills (e.g., prioritize work, complete tasks on time as promised, etc.)
5. Personal balance and development (e.g., exercise, leave office at a reasonable time, work fewer hours per day, spend more time with family, reduce travel, etc.)
6. Improve relationship with supervisor
7. Build a network with peers
8. Coach and mentor direct reports
9. Increase empathy
10. Increase organizational awareness
11. Improve conflict resolutions skills
12. Increase initiative
13. Be a better catalyst for change
14. Improve ability to build a high performing team

Challenges and potential pitfalls: determining and managing the boundaries for ourselves and our clients.

Working as a team with multiple coaches in an organization presents challenges for the coaches to manage the boundaries within ourselves, our team, and with our client. At the core of this issue, of course, are trust and confidentiality. We first had to build trust within our team. But even once trust was established among ourselves, we still each had to be mindful of how much we should share, because of how knowledge might influence our work. For example, there might be potential conflicts of interest between our coachees in vying for a promotion or a coveted role. In those instances, we chose not to share all the information with each other so as not to influence our fellow coaches' work with their coachees. Even if there were no obvious conflicts of interest involved, we naturally found that just having more information than we would ordinarily have when working with just one coachee could influence our work. For example, we noticed that we might be asking questions or probing further than we otherwise might have if we had not had such extensive knowledge of, and experience in, the organization.

On the other hand, there are obvious benefits of this information. For example, having organizational knowledge makes it possible to point out a potential resource to a coachee, such as support networks or other VPs who might have the knowledge and expertise to support our client that he or she might not have known. In our work, we travelled to many offices across the country, resulting in a greater breadth and depth of organizational knowledge than some of our coachees had, because they were often new officers in the company or worked primarily in one business unit or within a limited geography. It was possible for us to share our organizational knowledge with our coachee for their benefit.

One of the benefits of an external coach is that he or she is relatively independent of the politics of the organization and coachees usually feel freer to confide in the external coach. One benefit of an internal coach is their knowledge of the organization. Because of our extensive work with the client, we were able to offer the trust and confidentiality characteristic of an external coach along with some of the benefits ordinarily reserved for internal coaches, such as extensive knowledge of the organization.

During our quarterly coaching meetings, we typically discussed progress with our coachees as well as issues facing the organization. Our coachees had individual goals, but we were also interested in supporting the organization's goals of increased leadership and improved collaboration among the senior executives. We found ourselves being mindful of working with our clients on two levels, the individual and the organizational. There were times when our coachees improved a little too quickly for senior management. Sometimes the coachees' feedback to senior management and active participation in officer meetings was more than their superiors bargained for. And, of course, that was when we could intervene as organizational consultants to support management and assure them that senior executives speaking up in a constructive manner when they disagreed, rather than appearing to be silently in agreement when they were not, was in fact a positive development.

Another challenge, not so unique to our model and common to all coaching, is that sometimes there are conflicts between the company's interests and those of the coachees. A typical example is the company's need to relocate an executive. The executive accepts, but then has difficulty meeting the challenges of his or her new post. Sometimes a spouse is unhappy and sometimes it is the executive who might not feel up to the challenge of expanding new markets. Obviously, these are not simple black or white situations. It may appear that it is in the executive's best interest to return home, and this is in conflict with the company's interest. But are the company's interests served well by an executive who is unhappy or not up to the challenge? Sometimes the company's interests would be better served with a different executive leading the initiative. We had examples of both. In most cases, with some coaching and support, the executive was able to make the transition and meet his or her goals and commitments. In others, it was clear that the assignment was not a good match for the coachee's strengths and that neither the company nor the coachee was going to be successful. In those cases, coaching helped the individual work with supervisors to find a different role.

Another challenge of an external consultant working for a long time with a client is a tendency to identify or own the company's struggles. We sometimes caught ourselves saying "we" or "our" when referring to the company. In our individual work with our coachees, we noticed a tendency to take on their burdens and to be tempted to advocate for our client. Our team approach helped us to maintain our objectivity and boundaries with our client company and our individual clients. In this way, we were able to serve as checks and balances for each other.

Because our team of coaches worked together on this project for approximately seven years, we had learned our relative strengths as coaches. We could have discussions at the beginning of our new assignments regarding who would work best with which coachee. Our assignments always began with a debrief from the company's president, in which he provided a synopsis of each executive, including the executive's history with the company, his or her current role, and the company's performance expectations. Also, from our work in the company, we may have met the person before and had some first-hand knowledge of him or her, or the office or region in which the individual worked. This was extremely helpful in our making coaching assignments. Often, in coaching, an executive picks his or her coach after interviewing and meeting a few candidates. Our process of making coaching assignments was more driven by the coaches themselves, who were uniquely familiar with the structure and functioning of the company as well as the executives' coaching history.

The value and benefit of a team model for executive coaches

Although there are challenges and potential pitfalls of working as a team with more than one executive over time, there are several advantages for the individual coaches, the executives, and, ultimately, the company. As in the parable of the Blind Man and the Elephant, an individual coach is often in the position of not knowing the whole animal. A single coach may be hanging on to the tail and come to the conclusion that the tail is the nature of the business: long, bony, with a fur covering. The coach might also assume that he/she had hold of an "animal", but would not know which of the thousands of tailed animals it was. A team of coaches, able to communicate and share knowledge and experience, is able to feel its way from tail to head to more thoroughly and accurately determine which animal is actually in its grasp. Since we worked with our client for a period of seven years, in an ongoing leadership development programme, this broad scope created the unique opportunity for external consultants to become very knowledgeable, over time, about the company. Through hundreds of multi-rater interviews, shadowing, visiting offices throughout the nation, meetings with the CEO and the Organizational Learning Director, as well as direct coaching, our number of relationships multiplied. Getting to know the individual in the context of an organization, its culture, its business units, and various geographical locations gives a picture, again over time, of the "whole animal". With this systemic view, we were better able to understand the opportunities and challenges facing the firm's leaders.

As our team of coaches gained more knowledge about the company, we began to identify and discuss organizational factors that might be supporting or limiting the success of the firm's leadership development. With increased organizational awareness and understanding, we were better able to assist each executive to consider the organizational context when setting individual developmental goals and strategies.

An example where our organizational knowledge proved helpful was with an executive who had tried repeatedly to speak up and challenge the compensation review process. One of his developmental goals was to override his genial, conflict-avoidant style with a calm, assertive approach to conflict resolution. Each time he spoke up to the review group, he felt ignored and marginalized. Given our comprehensive understanding of the company's culture of favouring congeniality over openly and directly facing conflict, and our knowledge and grounding in group behaviour, his coach suggested an alternative route. He began to build an authentic one-on-one relationship with the head of the compensation group and practised over time a very effective influencing approach on the compensation review process. His success was personally gratifying and beneficial to others in the organization.

Some of the senior executives we coached were new to the company. It is always challenging to enter a new organization and culture at a senior level. The company often recruited these senior executives for their proven successful track record and slightly different approach, which might offer something new to the company. These executives often found difficulty in sharing their innovative approaches with the longer established employees of the company. Given our experience and knowledge of the company's culture, we could help the new executive navigate unfamiliar waters, build a peer network, identify resources, and integrate in a new and unfamiliar culture more easily.

Because of our general knowledge of the company, we could be more supportive and secure in our direction with our coachee. For instance, one coachee was unhappy living in an isolated geographic area that the company served. With support from his coach, he was able to investigate other possibilities that might better suit his need for peer interaction. Eventually, he found an office located in a growing market area that would utilize his experience and where he would also have a network of peers. The result was that he was less isolated and more successful, which benefited both him and the company overall.

Fostering collaboration among peers is a common problem in today's competitive, fast-paced organizations. We were often able to address competition and collaboration more easily than we might have, since we were working with more than one executive. In one instance, a coach happened to be working with three executives from different business units who resided in the same office. Although the office was small, the executives rarely collaborated, because they were more focused on their respective business units. The company wanted to encourage communication and collaboration across business units, which they hoped would facilitate sales through sharing information about a client's needs. So, when a coach came to work with one of the executives in this office, and because the coach had previously worked with the other two executives, they were able to arrange group lunch meetings to begin to foster communication and collaboration across business units. It was easier to get acceptance for the group lunch meetings since the coach knew all three executives and had a working relationship with each. It might have been more difficult to arrange if the coach had a relationship with only one of the individuals.

Resolving conflicts and promoting collaboration seemed easier when the coach had positive working relationships with an executive and his peers. A coach worked with two executives who were from different offices, but were within the same business and larger geographic unit. During the course of their work, the executives found themselves on opposite sides of a very important ethical issue. Both executives trusted the coach and asked the coach to facilitate a conflict resolution meeting between the two. After considerable discussion, the executives were able to find a common ground. It is possible that a similar outcome could have occurred with independent external coaches working solo, but that would probably have been less likely. Most probably, each would have been working independently with his or her coachee and the coach would not have had the opportunity to facilitate communication and collaboration between the executives. So, while there are pitfalls to be mindful of, there are many advantages to working as a team of coaches with multiple executives that benefit the coaching team, the executives, and the company.

Evaluating the programme's impact

Executive coaching programmes are a considerable investment of time and money (Wasylyshyn, 2003). Companies are always interested in the return on their investment. What was the outcome of all this effort? Since there are many factors that affect organizational performance, it is difficult to measure return on investment. Furthermore, from complexity theory we know that an action at one point sets a complex process in motion having consequences far removed from its origin (e.g., Stacey, 1996). The outcome measures we obtained were both empirical and observational. An independent consultant conducted an evaluation of the programme that included anonymous and confidential questionnaires to the coachees and interviews with the coaches. The data reported by the consultant were primarily self-reports by the coachees of the benefit of the programme. From the survey, the consultant reported that 89% of the former coachees reported a positive impact in their effectiveness as officers of the company as a result of the programme. Their self-report of improvement on a number of leadership competences was in the range of 75–90%. It is interesting to note that the primary benefit of the programme, as perceived by the majority of the former coachees, was improved self-awareness. They reported that they were more aware of their strengths and weaknesses. As a result of coaching, they reported that they were more aware of the daily choices they made and whether these helped or hindered them in achieving what they wanted as a leader. They also reported improvement in collaboration and team-work, competences the organization was interested in developing.

On an organizational and more macro level, there were also developments. Eric Miller taught that there are two criteria for change in an organization (Miller, 1959; Miller & Rice, 1967). An organization changes when it alters how it interacts with its environment and when there is an internal redistribution of power. From our observations, we observed both types of change in this organization. Regarding their responsiveness to the external environment, there were two organizational redesigns to meet client needs and changing market demands. Also, internal processes were being redesigned for more consistency and efficiency, so the company would be more competitive and better able to meet the needs of its clients. These were efforts to improve how they interacted with their external environment. Regarding redistribution of power, internally there were changes towards greater participation in how the company was governed. There was more participation from the officers at shareholder meetings. This seemed to be a result of efforts of the leaders as well as the executives. Giving and receiving feedback was more common practice. There was greater diversity in committee membership. There was also more tolerance and respect for diverging opinions. In an organizational culture that preferred to avoid conflict, there was a growing tolerance for differing opinions. There were also significant changes in the reward system. Ownership became less concentrated and more widely distributed. There are changes in rank *vs.* role that are still under way. Before, rank and role were synonymous; now they are being separated. It used to be that some roles were always performed by a Vice President; now that is not necessarily the case. These are some of the changes we have noted. At the end of each assignment, we continue to collect feedback. The reports continue to be positive. There are minor suggestions, for example, to make the programme longer, or to increase the frequency of contact, but, in general, the programme is viewed as beneficial. It is valued and seen as a significant way that the company invests in their development.

An exploration of next steps in developing
an individual and systemic model

What are the optimal mechanisms to use our confidential knowledge to further assist the organization in leadership development? Given the complete confidentiality of each coaching engagement, this is a challenge. Is there a way to further enhance the company's growth without violating confidentiality? Clearly, this would require modifying the model and our role without compromising the positive impact on the individual. Is it possible to provide organizational consultation without loss of value to the individual? Is it possible to share our organizational observations with senior management and still maintain trust and confidentiality with our individual coachees? In our work with this client, we have been asked many times by our coachees if we share our impressions of the company with senior leadership. Our coachees were interested in our impressions of the organization and, to our surprise, encouraged us to share our organizational insights with senior leadership, hoping this would have a positive impact for the company as a whole. Of course, this role would need to be negotiated and explicit at the beginning of the consulting assignment for clarity of roles and boundaries and confidentiality. The success of the consultation so far has been rooted in sound clinical practice by experienced psychologists, assurance of clear boundaries and confidentiality, independence from organizational politics, and broad appreciation of interpersonal and subjective processes. Its future must expand on these principals, rather than compromise them for any other goals or benefits. Our hope is to begin a dialogue with the senior management about the possibility of providing periodic feedback about the organization that would be helpful, but not violate the confidentiality of any individuals. Our team model for coaching approach demands mindfulness and sensitive collaboration among experienced consultants who are keenly aware of the needs of the organization, its executives, and each other.

References

Block, P. (1981). *Flawless Consulting: A Guide to Getting Your Expertise Used*. San Diego, CA: Pfeiffer.

Boyatzis, R., & McKee, A. (2005). *Resonant Leadership: Renewing Yourself and Connecting with Others through Mindfulness, Hope, and Compassion.* Boston, MA: Harvard Business School.

Boyatzis, R. E., Smith, M. L., & Blaize, N. (2006). Developing sustainable leaders through coaching and compassion. *Academy of Management Learning and Education, 5*(1): 8–24.

Fitzgerald, C. (2002). Understanding and supporting development of executives at midlife. In: C. Fitzgerald & J. G. Berger (Eds.), *Executive Coaching* (pp. 89–117). Palo Alto, CA: Davies-Black.

Goleman, D. (1998). *Working with Emotional Intelligence.* Bantam/Dell.

Goleman, D., Boyatzis, R. E., & McKee, A. (2002). *Primal Leadership: Realizing the Power of Emotional Intelligence.* Boston, MA: Harvard Business School Press.

Hackman, J. R. (2002). *Leading Teams: Setting the Stage for Great Performances.* Boston, MA: Harvard Business School.

Hackman, J. R., & Wegman, R. (2007). Coaching teams. Professional development workshop, Academy of Management, August.

Hay Group, with Boyatzis, R. E., & Goleman, D. (1999). *Emotional Competence Inventory.* Hay/McBer: www.haygroup.com/tl/Questionnaires_Workbooks/Emotional_Competency_Inventory.aspx

Hay Group, with Boyatzis, R. E., & Goleman, D. (2002). *Emotional Competence Inventory.* Hay/McBer: www.haygroup.com/tl/Questionnaires_Workbooks/Emotional_Competency_Inventory.aspx

Highlands Ability Battery (2004). New York.

Kampa-Kokesch, S., & Anderson, M. Z. (2001). Executive coaching: a comprehensive review of the literature. *Consulting Psychology Journal: Practice and Research, 53*(4): 205–228.

Kiel, F., Rimmer, E., Williams, K., & Doyle, M. (1996). Coaching at the top. *Consulting Psychology Journal: Practice and Research, 48*: 67–77.

Kilburg, R. R. (1996). Toward a conceptual understanding and definition of executive coaching. *Consulting Psychology Journal: Practice and Research, 48*: 134–144.

Miller, E. J. (1959). Technology, territory and time: the internal differentiation of complex production systems. *Human Relations, 12*: 243–272.

Miller, E., & Rice, K. (1967). *Systems of Organization.* London: Tavistock.

Stacey, R. D. (1996). Complexity and creativity in organizations. San Francisco, CA: Berret-Koehler.

Wasylyshyn, K. M. (2003). Executive coaching: an outcome study. *Consulting Psychology Journal: Practice and Research, 55*(2): 94–106.

Winum, P. C. (2003). Developing leadership: what is distinctive about what psychologists can offer? *Consulting Psychology Journal: Practice and Research, 55*(1): 41–46.

CHAPTER EIGHT

Integrating mindsets: a story of a role consultation between peers

Deborah Davidson and Libby Kinneen

Introduction

I n 2000 the Irish government produced a new health strategy *Quality and Fairness: A Health System for You* (2001). The strategy outlined the largest concentrated expansion in services in the history of the Irish health system and the consequent reform process represented the single biggest such change in the history of the state.

The structures in place for some thirty-five years were to be replaced. The new organizational structures included the establishment of the Health Service Executive (HSE) to enable the government to create a system better geared to meeting the many and complex tasks required of a modern health service.

The government set a demanding programme of work, identifying a number of key priorities to underpin their Health Service Reform Programme and the critical success factors for achieving organizational change. Their aim was to ensure that responsibility for delivering on various aspects of the strategy was made explicit and that implementation was achieved nationally in a consistent, effective, and timely manner. Outcomes would be monitored and evaluated over time and ongoing measurement and reporting of progress against the targets was seen as an essential part of the implementation process.

At regional level, the Health Boards—established under the Health Act (1970) for the administration of the health services in the state—were to be rationalized from eleven Health Boards to four HSE Regions, resulting in local redundancies and reassignments of many in senior managers' roles. This had a major organizational impact in a culture where the system was very personal: i.e., everyone knew everyone; many people were related; people would know most of the personal histories and background, including longstanding political allegiances.

These national changes had significant implications for the role and work of one existing Director of Organization Development (OD). Libby—who had worked for the same organization since 1979 (originally as a speech and language therapist)—had carved out an organizational development practitioner role for herself, working with all sectors of the health service and at many different levels, e.g., individuals, teams, larger scale interventions including socio-technical restructures, and more strategic management and senior level requests. The local impact of national changes prompted Libby to seek support in order to decide on whether and how to make the transition into a new role.

In May 2004, Libby approached Deborah to ask for consultation. This request was significant, as they both had been graduates of the same professional development programme, graduating at different times, and, as such, were peers. Libby explained that she was seeking support from someone who had knowledge of the kind of changes that might be anticipated in the Irish healthcare system, and wanted to learn about how healthcare organizations in England had responded to the challenge of service reform.

Libby identified her needs as wishing for "role" inputs to stretch herself further, get an external perspective, and find a source of more strategic focused literature/conceptual frameworks that would support her in this transition. She discussed using each session as a space to think about particular things (she would lead on this), and reflected on being pragmatic, reflective, and good at thinking on her feet (process) and wanted to use Deborah as a sounding board.

Deborah was concerned to ensure that there was a match between what "style" of consultation Libby wanted and what she could offer in terms of *how* she worked, and not just what content expertise she could bring to the discussions. The method she proposed using is called *role consultation*. Her conceptual framework is briefly explained below.

Through the perspectives of both client (Libby) and consultant (Deborah), this chapter explores the context, conceptual framework, and journey they took together over a period of three and half years. Working with key issues that emerged through these two lenses, we attempt to show how Libby's use of role consultation helped her to shape her role and develop the system she worked in. In doing so, we reflect on what we both learnt from this experience:

- how to explicitly work with the tensions that arise from different approaches and bias to change;
- strategizing and political thinking as key mechanisms in managing change;
- the influence of identity and values in role-taking;
- the value of corresponding and regular time-out to think;
- mindsets that might emerge when working as peers.

Role consultation: a conceptual framework

Consulting to role can take many forms, and is an intervention for unpacking and clarifying the complexity of work roles and work place situations (Armstrong, 1997; Hutton, Bazalgette, & Reed, 1994; Krantz & Maltz, 1997; Reed & Bazalgette, 2006). As a method, it is especially useful in enabling people to successfully make a significant transition into new roles.

Like coaching, role consultation provides an opportunity for a person to examine and explore the way in which they take up their role (*process*). Unlike mentoring, role consultation does not focus on providing "expert" advice (*content*) in relation to a given role, task area, or career development.

In this process, role consultation differs from both in that it examines and clarifies six factors of organizational role. The first four—*task*; *boundary*; *authority*; and *role-relationships* are derived from systems (Miller & Rice, 1967) and psychoanalytic thinking (Czander, 1993). The last two—connected to the core *purpose* of the organization (Reed & Bazalgette, 2006) and the *nature* of the work (Obholzer & Roberts, 1994)—are systemic concepts. (Some of the anxieties or key dilemmas in the system that are being expressed consciously or unconsciously; what one part of the system might be expressing on behalf of another, or why the rest of the system is helping to maintain a particular situation [Vega Roberts, personal communication, 2007].) These six *role factors*, within the context of the organization and its environment, provide an underlying frame of reference for the work. This is shown in Figure 1.

Observation of people's organizational experiences suggests that the interplay of these role factors can significantly determine the behaviour of the person in role (this view does not exclude the fact that a person's history and personality will also be factors in behaviour [Neumann, 2008]), their role-in-the-mind (a term adapted from Hutton, Bazalgette, and Reed [1994]) so to speak, and can influence the interactions of others with whom they come into contact. Being mindful of, and attending to, these components in a consultation means that workplace issues presented can be explored, thought about, and clarified in relation to these factors and (ideally) changes made.

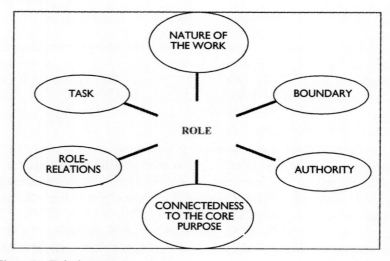

Figure 1.   Role factors.

Identity, meaning, and mindset

In most situations, however, exploration of these six factors alone is insufficient to address the issues faced. Taking up a role is predicated not only on an understanding and relatedness to the system one is in and its context, but also on how one identifies in role and the meaning that is assigned to this identity.

Stets and Burke (1998) state that, theoretically, the core of an identity is the categorization of the self as a role-holder, and the integration within oneself of the meanings and expectations associated with that role and the way it is performed (Burke & Tully, 1977; Thoits, 1983). These meanings and expectations form a set of standards that guide one's behaviour (Burke, 1991; Burke & Reitzes, 1981) and guide all the things that take on meaning in relation to our plans and activities (McCall & Simmons, 1978).

Deborah suggests that a tangible outcome of this isomorphic relationship (between identity and behaviour in role) is the construction of a *role mindset* that influences the perception of task, the decisions and actions taken, and governs the nature of the role relationships developed.

Given Libby's length of service, "self carved-out role", and her professional development in advanced organizational consultation, an organizational development mindset was likely to have a dominant influence on her sense of identity and inform her practitioner value base. However, Libby was moving from an *OD* practitioner role into an *executive* role, and entering and needing to engage with a *political process* that was located in a different part of the whole system. These challenges to identity and meaning meant that other mindsets needed to be consciously made available to enable Libby to manage this role and system transition as different situations emerged.

Although not necessarily part of the conceptual framework for role consultation, in this work a further theoretical frame was required in relation to political thinking.

Political thinking

Politics with a small "p" is inevitable in every organizational encounter, and, as Buchanan and Badham suggest, "plays a more significant role in organizational life than is commonly recognised" (2003, p. 1). They put forward that

> The so called "post modern" organization is characterised by fluidity, uncertainty, ambiguity and discontinuity . . . this fluid and shifting context implies an increased dependence on personal and inter-personal resources and on political skills to advance personal and organizational agendas. [*ibid*.]

Certainly Libby needed to engage with the inevitable shifting sands of national policy and practice and work with this in the process of both establishing a new role for herself and establishing a reconfigured OD service for her region. To do this meant introducing political thinking into her work. To support Libby's work with this, Deborah focused on, and used, three actions for thinking politically.

1. Constructing a way of getting things done that takes account of divergent interests and power differentials.
2. Working actively to shift the balance of power to further her desired agenda.
3. Limiting or deflecting the power and actions of others deliberately.

To this end, a key question that had to be kept in mind during Libby's work, against which actions and decisions were checked, was *what are the political forces at work here and to what extent have I taken them into account?*

A useful frame of reference for political thinking (devised by Deborah Davidson from research undertaken over a period of thirteen years while observing and consulting to individuals and groups in the public sector) is to be mindful of some or all of the following strategies.

1. Take account of wider and competing issues.
2. Locate where organisational power lies (individuals and groups).
3. Recognize the culture that underpins their "normal" way of operating.
4. Put oneself in the other's shoes (their interests and must do's).

5. Don't undermine their authority, status, and ego (which can often be very fragile).
6. Network proactively (political antennae to pick up information).
7. Think about and prepare for (inter)actions in order to articulate your thinking and take up your role.
8. Speak with authority (yours and others).
9. Create dependencies.
10. Suggestive coaching.

Method of working

Deborah usually begins by working with a person to map out their role, their relatedness to others, and what the organization looks like to them. This can be achieved either by talking about it or using an adaptation of a method called "organizational role analysis". Here, a person is encouraged literally to draw what the organization looks like, that is, their organization-in-the-mind (Armstrong, 1997; Carr, 1999; Reed, 1976; Reed & Bazalgette, 2006; Shapiro & Carr, 1991). This is their mental image of the organization (or a part of it) in its context with them in it, which is informing their experiences, shaping their behaviour, and influencing their work relations both overtly and covertly. This then begins to provide the material with which to work.

The material offered can be explored, questions asked, and observations made. Attention needs to be given to both the content and process described by the consultee as well as to the counter-transferential process (Little, 2003) between consultant and client. The aim is to enable the person to clarify those aspects of their work/work relations that seem to cause problems or frustrate them, and to help them find ways of resolving those issues. Sessions (content and process) also are reflected upon and reviewed from both client and consultant perspectives, for learning and improvement.

In the next section, we tell a three-part story, focusing on some key issues that emerged to exemplify how we worked, the ways in which this helped Libby to manage an effective transition for herself and for the system, and reflect on the usefulness of role consultation as a method.

Getting started

Libby's experience

At the start of the consultation process, I was a well-established internal consultant with a real sense of self as an OD practitioner. I had strong authority in the old system in terms of role, position, expertise, and felt very connected to the work, having a good knowledge of the system in which I worked.

I became aware that "my" system was about to change dramatically in terms of structure, culture, and task, and I needed to start preparing for the changes ahead. It was in this context that I sought role consultation to assist me in the process, and chose a consultant who had knowledge and experience of the kind of major reform the Irish Health Service was undergoing. I had a strong apprehension that the reform agenda was going to have a big impact on how I was going to be able to take up my role.

I had some anxiety about whether my normative-re-educative approach to change (Chin & Benne, 1961) would be valued in the new system. I was in an environment where old systems and structures were being actively dismantled at a rapid rate.

Initially, I had considered applying for the position of National Director of Organizational Development, but decided against this. Later, as the changes became real, major structural changes took place in the health service as a whole and the OD function specifically, including the transfer of OD from an independent function to a sub-unit of the National HR function. I did not get the opportunity to be part of this decision-making process, which resulted in strong feelings of depression, anger, powerlessness, and anxiety. At the lowest point, I felt I would have to leave the system if I was to survive as an organizational consultant, practising in the way I had been trained. I spent some time exploring leaving the organization and possible options outside the health service.

Although some of this period was extremely difficult, role consultation provided me with a sense of containment that enabled me not only to survive, but to think through the necessary negotiations for a new role as Area Head of Organization Development and Design. Deborah introduced me to the notion of transitional space (Winnicott, 1971) and assisted me to explore my approach to organizational politics. I found this both thought-provoking and disturbing, as I had always kept some distance from this. The intervention proved to be very effective in prompting me to attend more to this area.

What I found particularly useful during this period was the use of concepts, e.g., needing to focus on anticipatory and reactive processes of change, understanding the interface between OD and policy implementation, scoping how to market myself in a highly political environment. We also spent some time discussing specific consultancy projects that not only supported my professional development, but also helped to ground me as well as bridge the gap between the old and newly emerging role.

Deborah's focus

During this early phase, I sought to explore the extent and character of Libby's system-in-the mind (Hutton, Bazalgette, & Reed, 1994). The initial mapping was difficult to follow. New appointments at governmental level were being made, transitional structures for different strands of work were being established, and appointments from existing and new sources were announced. However, structures, functions, and roles—both old and new—seemed to merge across national, regional, and local boundaries into a confused mass (in my mind, at least). It took some time for this whole system picture to become clear. My confusion seemed to be a countertransference (Halton, 1994) of the system's experience.

Three things did emerge clearly from this mapping, which were foci for the role consultation: (i) reframing the task; (ii) appreciating the political character of the wider system; (iii) deciding whether, and how, to work with this change.

Reframing the task

Libby's identity was as an organizational development practitioner and this strongly influenced the way in which she defined her day-to-day tasks and the approaches she took when working with the system. Her preference for a normative–re-educative approach (Chin & Benne, 1961) meant that she saw as essential the involvement and participation of those affected by change in the system. Central to this was enabling people to have some ownership and control over the change. This organizational development practitioner mindset influenced the way Libby initially responded to the change happening to herself, and could potentially have been viewed by those above her as resistance.

Reform to the health service precipitated at a national level (top-down) seemed to be more rational–empirical (statements about what needs to happen and why, with an expectation that the necessary actions would follow) and power–coercive (change based on the exercise of authority and the imposition of sanctions if instructions are not followed) (Chin & Benne, 1961), two strategies commonly found in public service systems. Focusing on these preferred strategies for change brought into view the idea that the task needed to be conceptualized differently; it was not organizational development but *policy implementation* that was being asked of Libby. The requisite mindset for this task was a political one. Bringing into view a political mindset (Figure 2) could open up the potential for seeing the task from the standpoint of politicians and senior civil servants, charged with system reform.

This seemed to enable Libby to better appreciate the political character of the wider system in which she was an actor. In particular, to recognize the culture that underpinned the "normal" way of operating at a national level and to put herself in their shoes.

Appreciating the political character of the wider system

Libby had alluded to a system of relationships that seemed personal, with long-standing political allegiances that had the potential to influence interim appointments, decision-making, and transitional structures. Over the course of her work, Libby had various contacts and relationships with some of these people, but for others was unknown. Both the previous role relationships and her invisibility would have a bearing on the ways in which she was perceived and the nature of engagement. Libby was keen to think

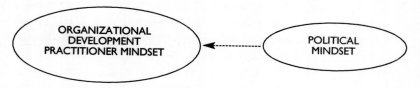

Figure 2. Bringing into view a political mindset.

through how to operate at a national level and become more influential.

Navigating in a political environment requires political thinking and skill. In particular, locating where organizational power lies, networking proactively to pick up information and influence the change, and most importantly, ensuring that any decisions and actions don't undermine the authority of superiors.

However, this did not mean giving up Libby's preferred approaches, nor leaving negative impacts of national approaches unchallenged. Instead, it meant integrating mindsets (Figure 3) to consider what strategies and tactics were required to retain and influence—as far as possible—normative–re-educative approaches at national, regional, and local levels.

A key strategy at this stage was to find ways of supporting national actors charged with implementing change at regional and local levels in order to role model system change using normative–re-educative principles.

Deciding whether, and how, to work with this change

Underpinning these deliberations were other fundamental questions that needed addressing. Did Libby want to stay and work with this change? Did she want a strategic role in this reformed system? Would she be able to make the transition to a national and strategic level?

These questions took many months to be answered fully as Libby worked through a process of loss and change (Marris, 1993). A starting point for this was thinking about two key elements—her motivation and energy, and the need to have some control over her future. I drew upon the Grubb Institute's "Framework for transforming experience" (which is discussed in Reed & Bazalgette, 2006) in this work with Libby.

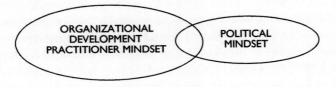

Figure 3.   Integrating mindsets.

This framework was helpful in bringing a consciousness to the question "for whose purpose am I making this decision or taking this action?" and to illuminate how possible or difficult it was to act for the benefit of the system, in context. Realizing that her personal motivations were aligned with the purpose of the system enabled Libby to appreciate a third position (Benjamin, 1998; Tillett, 1994), that of the national and political contexts within which she needed to work if she were to make the transition into a new role.

Having decided that she did want to stay and negotiate a role, Libby then wanted to think through how to influence what this would look like. Recognizing that the pace of change would not stand still, but that the structure and roles were not fully determined, Libby sought to adopt a strategy of anticipatory change (where change is initiated in advance of future events to improve the competitive edge and where it is possible to choose a range of options for development and/or expansion) rather than reactive change (changes made in direct response to an external event, in some way "forced' upon the organization and often limited to a narrow range of choices) (Mohrman et al., 1989) for herself.

Strategizing and preparing for interactions became a key mechanism in managing the transition into a new role and in maintaining a normative re-educative approach in her work.

Making progress

Libby's experience

Around the time I was appointed Area Head of Organization Development and Design (it was only a few months since taking up my role), I was still focusing on adjusting political and organizational development mindsets and honing my political skills, i.e., responding, scanning, planning. Both Deborah and I noted that I was much happier in role, and working better with political processes, trying to shape them where possible, while attending to my own needs. I did this by spending much more time preparing and planning. This was reflected in the role consultation sessions, several of which were spent rehearsing for important meetings and interactions.

More clarity was available at a national level in terms of structure and roles, tasks were being allocated to individuals, and there seemed good scope for me to negotiate for work that interested and stimulated me, and which made sense in terms of my contribution and approach.

I used the role consultation sessions to focus more on the system than on my role, in particular the OD function and the many things I needed to consider, e.g., balancing time in terms of old/new projects, national and local work, use of people and resources across the system, and my role locally in the HSE. I was beginning to become aware of my role as an executive in the region. This involved letting go part of the consultancy role I had practised for many years.

Deborah's focus

I remember the consultation session after Libby successfully negotiated her new role as Area Head of Organization Development and Design very clearly.

Libby seemed settled, emotionally lighter, intellectually sprightly, and focused on what she needed to do. Central to this shift seemed to be the fact that she had negotiated a role that balanced both given and taken authorities and responsibilities (Krantz & Maltz, 1997), had been able to continue using a normative–re-educative approach in her practice, and had successfully "marketed" herself on a national stage.

This liberation and purposefulness pervaded a number of subsequent sessions, and enabled Libby to shift more of her focus to the system and the regional and local OD function. As Libby stated above, the system became more prominent at this stage, and she worked on how to conceptualize tasks, boundaries, and role relationships in connection with the regional and local OD functions.

It was during one particular session, when Libby discussed at length the complexity of working with a virtual OD function at local and regional levels, that an insight emerged, which brought into view a third required mindset. Libby was pondering how to get people at local levels to work to a wider strategic brief that she was developing for the region as a whole. Acutely aware of the personal relationships and long-standing political allegiances, and the fact that she did not have line management authority over them, she was concerned not to alienate colleagues, while nevertheless wanting to move them towards working together as a virtual system. Her suggestions as to how to tackle this centred on how she might "consult" to these people, to help move things on.

This raised a question as to how professional identity might still be influencing the way Libby was taking up her role. To date, the OD "practitioner" role had taken centre stage. Libby had "carved out an organizational development practitioner role for herself, working with all sectors of the health service . . .". However, Libby's new role was no longer as OD practitioner, but as an executive of the HSE, overseeing the management of a (virtual) OD function, and requiring her to manage this system and its range of resources. While Libby might draw upon an OD approach to inform her management practice, she was no longer just consulting to them as an OD practitioner. The requisite mindset for this task was an executive one (Figure 4).

The need for an executive mindset was again apparent at a later session when Libby discussed her role at the regional HSE. With a leadership vacuum, a series of local strategic roles had been appointed to cover functions such as Primary and Community Care, HR, Finance, and Hospital Care.

However, while undertaking an executive role on behalf of the national HSE at a local level, Libby—as the only woman at this level—had not been appointed as a board member. Instead, she had been invited to alternative meetings to be kept informed and was asked to consult to various activities as and when they arose.

As long as Libby conceptualized her role as an OD practitioner (albeit to a wider system), she was "unconsciously" colluding with the system to obliterate the OD function and make her own role invisible. Bringing into view and integrating an executive mindset allowed for a different professional identity to be thought about

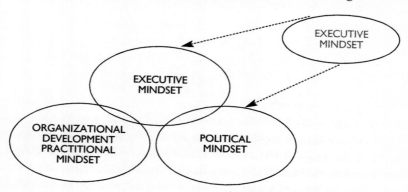

Figure 4.   Bringing into view and integrating an executive mindset.

and a different role taken up. While the leadership vacuum meant that Libby's role at regional HSE level would not change immediately, she could take steps to be more visible and function as a board member over time.

Institutionalizing the change

The third part of this story is unwritten, as Libby sets off to create her-story. (This feminist format for writing history is deliberately used as a play on words—it is both Libby's story to be created and it will be her history.) Over a period of three and a half years, a number of transitions were anticipated, prepared for, and made. One of these transitions was the ending of our role consultation relationship. This process took place—implicitly—over some months. In hindsight, ending became explicit when we agreed to write about our experience of working together and later when Libby began training in coaching, because it marked a shift in our relating, with the "peer" aspect of our relationship becoming more prominent.

Working more as peers, our reflections on the consultation experience became more explicit and available. This seemed a necessary step in Libby's future, because, in the process of ending, the many positive aspects from of the consultation experience are sufficiently internalized as part of the "separation and mourning process" (Loewald, 1962, 2000) and it is this process that enables Libby to meet and work with what follows with confidence.

Learning from client and consultant experiences: implications for practice

Working incrementally over fifteen consultations and a period of three and a half years made it difficult to pin-point all our learning, although key transitions and events remained alive. So we used those transitions and events, and drew out some aspects that may be of interest to others working with individuals through processes of role transition and change in a political system, including frameworks and tools which proved useful in the consultation.

Explicitly working with different approaches and bias to change

Role consultation proved to be extremely valuable in terms of providing both space and time to consider how to create and "take" a new role (Krantz & Maltz, 1997) in a highly political and turbulent system.

Libby learned to work with her passion and values so that she could influence key stakeholders positively, and not alienate them by challenging them about their approaches and asserting her approach as the "right" way. This came about by working on how to take up authority while staying true to her values, how to speak out and remain safe, how to model a developmental process while meeting national and political requirements. Our work together helped Libby to find within herself a different repertoire to deal passionately and constructively with events as they unfolded.

The consultation also provided Libby with the opportunity to distil her personal experiences, thereby gaining valuable insights that have had a direct impact on her own consultancy practice in terms of diagnostics and intervention, e.g., dealing with imposed organizational change requires different interventions than change that is chosen, and never underestimate the impact of change on individuals.

Strategizing and political thinking as key mechanisms for managing change

Drawing on concepts from large-scale organizational change— anticipatory and reactive change (Mohrman et al., 1989)—gave Libby a conceptual tool that she could apply to her situation. She used this well by working in anticipation of the change, actively thinking through potential scenarios, exploring situations from different perspectives (how are they right?) and debating the consequences of different paths of action.

A key tool in this process was asking the question "what are the political forces at work here and to what extent have I taken them into account?" Deborah used this question and two of the political thinking strategies regularly in her enquiry with Libby.

First, not undermining the authority, status, and ego (which can often be very fragile) of national players by checking on proposed decisions and actions, particularly when it came to discussing organizational development and change.

Appointments to national roles are short term because they come with enormous expectations to deliver political promises and meet head-on a system that does not want to work with those changes. The early stages in public service reform are particularly charged with expectations of individual heroes and heroines whose appointments as transformational leaders (Alimo-Metcalfe & Alban Metcalfe, 2003) are made on the basis of past successes that are expected to be reproduced. This context can lead to fragility in the role-holders, who need to be seen to deliver (by those above) and need to be seen as knowing what they are doing (by those below). In this context, it is enormously powerful to have greater sapiential authority (wisdom [the application of knowledge] gained through experience) than one's superiors, particularly in relation to change processes.

This links with the second political thinking strategy Deborah used: creating dependencies. For Libby this meant tactical use of her sapiential authority, by asking the question "how can I be of help to you in your dilemma?" and thinking through what it is she genuinely had to offer that would be helpful, which would also give her the opportunity to suggest a process of change and model her preferred approach.

The influence of identity and values in role-taking

The centrality of identity and values and their influence in role-taking was not intellectually surprising, but felt striking when working together. The depth of Libby's feelings, and her sense of having to leave work for her identity to survive, were powerful and overwhelming.

At the core of this was her articulation of the need to "practise in the way I had been trained", which seemed to refer to both her professional trainings, first as a speech and language therapist and then as an organizational consultant. These trainings share a common value that was explicit, that is enabling people—whether patients or clients—to have some ownership of, and choice and control over, the change that is affecting their lives.

Unravelling and articulating explicitly the values and beliefs that govern the way in which we construct our identity and engage with the world was important in setting a clear boundary, but not so rigidly that it denied a process of loss and change and closed down thinking. Paradoxically, we found that as Libby became clearer in her sense of self, this seemed to open up the space to think about how others might construct and engage differently, and how to work with those differences.

The value of corresponding and regular "time out" to think

The process of change in the system initially took a long time to be clarified and become sufficiently settled. The protracted negotiation in relation to structures and roles was stressful. Without the neces- sary support, major organizational change can lead to severe mental distress for those involved (Cartwright & Cooper, 1994). Certainly, at times, the stress of these changes had its impact on Libby. Role consultation was experienced as valuable, because it provided a corresponding regular opportunity and time out to think.

The structure of regular opportunities to think about what was happening and consider what to do meant that there was not a necessity to find solutions or move to actions too quickly. In this way, we were able to work alongside the transition as it happened and work through the inevitable loss.

In addition, time out from work, enabled Libby to stand back and look in at the situation. Her wish to use Deborah as a sound- ing board—sounding off and sounding out—created a distance that was containing for the anxieties and angers that arose out of Libby's experience, and avoided her bringing them into the workplace.

Conclusion: working as peers

We could not conclude this chapter without reflecting on our expe- rience of working together as peers, and it seems particularly perti- nent to think how this experience might inform others who have to work with close colleagues and people who know them well.

While editing this chapter, Karen Izod raised a very useful question: "I was confused as to why you regarded yourselves as peers and got into relating as peers?"

In hindsight, the answer seems obvious, but eluded us in our work together. While neither of us arrived at the consultation with the sense of "peer" in mind, a similar work environment, shared professional development approach, and a fantasy of the other's expertise influenced the dynamics that were going on between us in relation to the taking up of roles. Unconsciously, we contracted as peers.

Recognizing this has helped us to think through and articulate four "mindsets" that, together, might allow for fallibility and expertise on both sides of the consulting and client relationship when working as peers or close colleagues:

Exposed mindset: in peer and close working relationships, working as consultant and client can raise anxieties about both incompetence being exposed to someone whose opinion one values, and the competence of the other.

Libby

What worked well for both of us was having a shared professional development, which meant we had a common language and shared frameworks to work with. However, at the start I had not thought of myself as being in a peer relationship.

Not knowing Deborah beforehand meant I came with less preconceived notions—because I had never met her, my identity was very much as the client.

Deborah

From the beginning, I felt very clear that Libby was an experienced organizational consultant. Although I thought of us as peers, I did not feel as a peer because I was anxious about what on earth I could offer Libby, given her experience!

Managing my need to feel I had some thing to offer was around for me in the early stages.

Libby

On reflection, I wondered whether more formal contracting after the scouting conversation would have helped me to relinquish my need to be a peer.

Deborah

I think that Libby was right. For me, thinking as a peer in the early stages served to undermine my taking up of the role of consultant and working effectively through the contracting process. In previous work I had negotiated a formal agreement about how we would work and my expectations that we review our work every fourth session. I seemed to forget all of that with Libby, and was reminded again when she suggested we might review the content and process of our work at the end of each session as well as review where we had got to.

Socio-psychological mindset: during the contracting and early phases of work, it is important to attend to the socio-psychological aspects of role taking and task expectations. Being peers can obfuscate mindfulness of roles for both consultant and client.

Libby

I noticed a recurring theme in Deborah checking if the work we were doing was helpful, and wondered if my just wanting to use her as a sounding board rather than get specific advice made it more difficult for her to know if the consultation was helpful. Later in the process I became more open and started using Deborah's expertise in a different way; one might say it was when I stopped seeing it as a peer consultation, I became more open to other things on offer.

Wounded healer mindset: in peer and close working relationships, both the challenge of helping the competent *and (unconsciously) reluctant client are processes that need to be consciously worked with.* (The terms *competent* and *reluctant client* are from personal communication with Karen Izod (2008) and relate to material used on the Tavistock Institute's "Coaching for Leadership and Professional Development Programme", of which she is Co-Director.)

Deborah

As our work progressed, I was aware that my anxiety about being able to effectively consult to Libby might manifest itself in my taking up the "expert consultant" role (Block, 2000) as a means to managing my anxiety. As I worked to manage this, I was able to relinquish the need to be an expert and find and use my expertise in role. I was also able to entertain the idea that Libby might be anxious as a client. Taking up my role effectively seemed to have a simultaneous impact on Libby being able to relinquish the "peer" role and take up a client role.

Mutual engagement mindset: Seeing the consultant role and task as mutual engagement (Block, 2000) *enables the consultant to explicitly work with client expertise and be open to learning from the client in the process.*

Libby

As the consultation progressed, and my sense of identity became stronger and confidence in my ability to take up my role increased, Deborah's consultancy style enabled me to draw on my experiences and skills in the new context. This helped me speak to issues, drawing on my own competence. It again felt more like a peer relationship.

During one consultation, I suggested we might review the content and process of our work at the end of each session, and that periodically we evaluate the work overall. I felt I had touched some anxiety. Evaluation as part of the ongoing process proved to be very useful in the consultation, particularly in the peer context, as it gave us a framework to speak to process issues as well as keep track of shifts and changes.

Deborah

Libby raising the idea of evaluation also raised some of my old anxieties. What would she say about my practice and her experience of working with me? For me, this seemed more of an issue with a peer than it had been with other clients where evaluation was a regular feature of our work.

Despite these anxieties, I was able to work with Libby's ideas because they were important for our work together, and enabled another shift to take place in our relationship and trust. This brought to mind Patrick Casement's book *On Learning from the Patient* (2004) and his suggestion that we can monitor the implications of our own contributions from the viewpoint of the patient.

Running through each of these mindsets are the reciprocal roles (Ryle & Kerr, 2004) that are taken up by the actors; the role taken up by one evokes a reciprocal response from the other. The dance that is played out between the evoking and the taking up of the role can be led by either person in the consulting relationship. Being attuned to what gets evoked and played out between consultant and client—by listening with the third ear (Roberts, 2005, p. 112)— helps the consultant to be mindful in her practice.

References

Alimo-Metcalfe, B., & Alban Metcalfe, J. (2003). Stamp of greatness. *Health Service Journal, 113*(5861): 28–32.

Armstrong, D. G. (1997). The institution-in-the-mind: reflections on the relation of psychoanalysis to work with institutions. *Free Associations, 7*(1, 41): 1–14.

Benjamin, J. (1998). *Shadow of the Other: Intersubjectivity and Gender in Psychoanalysis* (3rd edn). London: Routledge.

Block, P. (2000). *Flawless Consulting: A Guide to Getting Your Expertise Used* (2nd edn). San Francisco, CA: Jossey-Bass/Pfeiffer.

Buchanan, D., & Badham, R. (2003). *Power, Politics and Organisational Change*. London: Sage.

Burke, P. J. (1991). Identity processes and social stress. *Sociological Review, 56*: 836–849.

Burke, P.J., & Reitzes, D. C. (1981). The link between identity and role performance. *Social Psychology Quarterly, 44*(2): 83–92.

Burke, P. J., & Tully, J. (1977). The measurement of role/identity. *Social Forces, 55*: 881–897.

Carr, W. (1999). Can we speak of spirituality in institutions? In: J. F. Cobble & C. M. Elliot (Eds.), *The Hidden Spirit* (pp. 109–117). Matthews, NC: CMR Press.

Cartwright, S., & Cooper, C. L. (1994). The human effects of mergers and acquisitions. In: C. L. Cooper & D. M. Rousseau (Eds.), *Trends in Organizational Behaviour* (Vol. 1, pp. 49–61). New York: Wiley.

Casement, P. (2003). *On Learning from the Patient*. Hove: Brunner-Routledge.

Chin, R., & Benne, K. D. (1961). General strategies for effecting change in human systems. In: W. G. Bennis, K. D. Benne, & R. Chin (Eds.), *The Planning of Change* (pp. 12–35). London: Holt, Rinehart & Winston.

Czander, W. M. (1993). *The Psychodynamics of Work and Organisations: Theory and Application*. London: Guilford.

Department of Health and Children (1970). *The Health Act*. Dublin: The Stationery Office.

Department of Health and Children (2001). *Quality and Fairness: A Health System for You*. Dublin: The Stationery Office.

Halton, W. (1994). Some unconscious aspects of organizational life: contributions from psychoanalysis. In: A. Obholzer & V. Z. Roberts (Eds.), *The Unconscious at Work: Stress in the Human Services* (pp. 11–18). London: Routledge.

Hutton, J., Bazalgette, J., & Reed, B. D. (1994). Organisation-in-the-mind. In: J. E. Neumann, K. Kellner, & A. Dawson-Shepherd (Eds.), *Developing Organisational Consultancy* (pp. 113–126). London: Routledge.

Krantz, J., & Maltz, M. (1997). A framework for consulting to organizational role. *Consulting Psychology Journal: Practice and Research, 49*: 137–151.

Little, M. (2003). Counter-transference and the patient's response to it. In: A. Furman & S. T. Levy (Eds.), *Influential Papers from the 1950s*. *International Journal of Psychoanalysis*, Key Paper Series. London: Karnac.

Loewald, H. (1962). Internalization, separation, mourning, and the superego. In: *Papers on Psychoanalysis* (pp. 257–276). New Haven, CT: Yale University Press, 1980.

Marris, P. (1993). *Loss and Change* (2nd edn). London: Routledge.

McCall, G. J., & Simmons, J. L. (1978). *Identities and Interactions*. New York: Free Press.

Miller, E. J., & Rice, A. K. (1967). *Systems of Organisation: The Control of Task and Sentient Boundaries*. London: Tavistock.

Mohrman, A. M., Mohrman, S. A., Ledford, G. E., Cummings, T. G., Lawler, E. E., & Associates (Eds.) (1989). *Large-Scale Organizational Change*. San Francisco. CA: Jossey-Bass.

Neumann, J. E. (2008). Consultant domain and client agenda. Paper presented to the Academy of Management Annual Meeting, Anaheim, CA, August.

Obholzer, A., & Roberts, V. Z. (Eds.) (1994). *The Unconscious At Work: Individual and Organisational Stress in the Human Services.* London: Routledge

Reed, B. D. (1976). Organizational role analysis. In: C. L. Cooper (Ed.), *Developing Social Skills in Managers: Advances in Group Training* (pp. 89–102). London: Macmillan.

Reed, B. D., & Bazalgette, J. (2006). Organizational role analysis at the Grubb Institute of Behavioural Studies: origins and development. In: J. Newton, S. Long, & B. Sievers (Eds.), *Coaching in Depth: The Organizational Role Analysis Approach* (pp. 43–62). London: Karnac.

Ryle, A., & Kerr, I. B. (2005). *Introducing Cognitive Analytic Therapy: Principles and Practice.* Chichester: Wiley.

Roberts, V. Z. (2005). Psychodynamic approaches: organisational health and effectiveness. In: E. W. Peck (Ed.), *Organisational Development in Healthcare: Approaches, Innovations, Achievements* (pp. 101–126). Oxford: Radcliffe.

Shapiro, E., & Carr, W. (1991). *Lost in Familiar Places: Making New Connections Between Individual and Society.* New Haven, CT: Yale University Press.

Stets, J. E., & Burke, P. J. (1998). Identity theory and social identity theory. Paper presented to the meeting of the American Sociological Association, San Francisco, CA.

Thoits, P. A. (1983). Multiple identities and psychological well-being. *American Sociological Review, 49*: 174–187.

Tillett, R. (1994). The clinical usefulness of gestalt therapy. *British Journal of Psychotherapy, 11*(2): 290–297.

Winnicott, D. W. (1971). *Playing and Reality,* London: Penguin.

CHAPTER NINE

Energy world: developing the accountancy profession for ethical leadership[1]

Kevin Dixon

Introduction

I am passionate about learning, and effective consultation. I can trace my ideas on energy and developing ethical leadership to my self-review at the end of the Tavistock Institute's MA in Advanced Organizational Consultation (AOC) and my dissertation (Dixon, 2004). It was then that I identified learning themes across science, art and money, finding meaning from different fields. It emerged, for me, that to be an effective consultant I required change.

In April 2005, I left the UK's Civil Service and started my own private consultancy practice (Cross Boundary Solutions Ltd). As a senior internal consultant, I had worked closely with top leaders and was involved in the successful implementation of new accounting and budgeting systems across government in the UK and Ireland. Subsequently, I helped to develop proposals for government to set up a leadership centre for the voluntary and community sector in England, which ultimately failed. This chapter emanates from the development of my consultancy practice since then.

In January 2006, as an aid to my coaching, I became qualified by the British Psychological Society to administer and provide feedback on level "A" (ability) and level "B" (personality) psychometric instruments. I was interested in taking my coaching further, and had developed an approach "Authentic Leadership Coaching" (AuthENtic) that utilizes the core energy for fast-track learning: Authorised and acknowledged; Unique and understood; Targeted and respected; Holistic; ENERGIZED; Trusted; Integrated and Confidential. As part of my experimentation, I invited a fellow consultant, who had reached a crossroads in her career and life, to accompany me on a trip to Morocco to experience the contrast of the cool Riad, and the noisy exuberant vitality of the souks of Djemaa el Fina square, in the red city of Marrakech. The square bustles with acrobats, story-tellers, orange juice sellers, dancers, and musicians by day and night.

We were in a group of ten, led by an English travel guide, and spent five days in the desert. Sleeping in black cloth tents, organized in different formations each night by the blue-clad Berbers, we had travelling conversations on "dancing camels", exchanging images as we sailed up and down magnificent sand dunes of the Western Sahara. The trip was a big success, and my colleague felt she had been hugely refreshed by the experience.

Following this unique calm, in Africa, on the boundary with Europe, with leaders that I describe as exhibiting signs of "burnout", I brought together consultants with different consulting domains at a hotel in London, with "energy" as the focus of the experience. The results of that workshop are described here, and the outcomes used to inform the proposed intervention with the accountancy profession.

Building on earlier conversations, in October 2006 I was invited by an American-based company to learn the instrument "Focus Energy Balance Indicator" (FEBI), which can be used to locate an individual's personal home "energy" for self-awareness and team-building in organizations.

In January 2007, I took a trip to India, partly to stay on an Ashram in Pondicherry to begin study of an integrated form of yoga (Mukherjee, 2003). I had studied Yoga in my mid-twenties, run seven marathons in my mid-forties and have a diploma in holistic healing. I wanted to re-engage with my personal energy and reflect upon my learning.

Meanwhile, as Treasurer of the Advanced Organizational Consultation Society, Trustee of a UK-wide charity, I continued to use my experience as an accountant and leader. While these activities have provided me with substantial learning that has informed my practice, I focus here on my experience in dealing with money, with my consultancy practice in the foreground.

An identified need

This chapter consults to an identified need (International Federation of Accountants [IFAC], 2007) to develop ethical training in the accountancy profession. I also propose that this intervention can build upon work done by leaders of the profession (Consultancy Committee of Accountancy Bodies [CCAB], 2006). I refer here to "leaders" as accountants in leadership positions. Ethical leaders are leaders who act on high moral standards: head, heart, and guts (courage) (Dotlich, Cairo, & Rhinesmith, 2006): they are "leaders-in-action", rather than "espoused" leaders (Argyris & Schön, 1974). I assume that "good" acts can be learnt from the "bad" (Kellerman, 2004). I relate the "good" and "bad" in character to the "unifying confluence" of the "depressive position" (Hinshelwood, 1989) as a sense of loss in "healthy and mature" individuals and organization.

My aim is to engage with the accountancy profession. I offer this learning, presented here in three suggested modalities: experientially; vicariously through story-telling, drama, role play, and simulation; and visually through art. I use the metaphor of a prism to illuminate ethical dilemmas and judgement in the context of a confluence of learning as change. I see art as being resistant to standardized control, a way of developing sentient meaning, and finding energy and passion for what has been lost.

Ethical challenges identified by the profession

There are two main bodies that affect ethical training of accountants in the UK and Ireland. These are the International Federation of Accountants (IFAC) International Ethics Standards Board for

Accountants (IASBA) and the Consultative Committee of Accountancy Bodies (CCAB) Ethics Education Forum (EEF). IFAC has an International Accounting Standards Board (IASB) and the CCAB has an Accounting Standards Board (ASB). As part of plans for general global convergence in accounting rules and regulations, the ASB is gradually adopting the practices of the IASB. The following statement expresses the shared aims of those bodies:

> To serve the public interest by setting high quality ethical standards for professional accountants and by facilitating the convergence of international and national ethical standards thereby enhancing the quality and consistency of services provided by professional accountants. [IFAC, 2007]

In September 2006, the International Ethnics Standards Board for Accountants (IESBA) established a four-stage learning continuum, with learning outcomes and a description of competence required for each stage. The four stages are:

- enhancing ethics knowledge;
- developing ethical sensitivity;
- improving ethical judgement;
- maintaining an ongoing commitment to ethical behaviour (*ibid.*).

Also recommended were a number of teaching methods: lectures, peer-led discussions, case studies, and examples of ethical threats, role-play, and E-learning. At a meeting in London towards the end of 2006, it was agreed that it is important to cover all four stages of ethics education as part of a professional accountant's education and to revisit the stages throughout an accountant's career. Subsequent Ethic Education Forum (EEF) reports highlight the need for "sharing real-life ethical threats and challenges" (International Education Practice Statement 1 [IEPS 1], 2006, p. 10).

Environmental challenges

Recent world-wide market volatility, increasing energy resource inflation, over-valued housing, high credit, and the government (taxpayer) bail-out of a High Street bank, are examples of potential further collapse of confidence in regulation, ethical behaviour, and judgement: "An important asset of the modern corporation is its expected future earning capacity determined by social expectations about the future" (Raines & Leathers, 1996). Because corporate value is influenced by social perception, the foundations of the corporate economy are fundamentally prone to manipulation (Hake, 2005).

If accountants do not use their judgement wisely, consumers will not trust earnings forecasts, work will lose meaning and motivation, and confidence and spending will decline. As a result, accountancy bodies have specifically identified that they need to develop skills in leadership, decision making, trust building, communication, and conflict management by exposing students to "ethical threats"; the development of critical thinking and reflective learning skills; and the integration of technical skills and knowledge with ethical decision-making frameworks. The accountant needs to be prepared to go to these dark places, to feel the connection between the material and the non-material, so that emotions are switched on.

In the long-term, recession might not be considered a "bad thing" if people learn to live on less money and seek value in spiritual rather than material ends, with respect for ethical behaviour.

The prism

Coming from a large country family supported by a small family business, I grew up with a strong sense of family and work ethic. When I was three years old, I stayed with my grandparents for a few days while my mother was giving birth to my younger brother, and was given a glass prism by my grandfather. I held the prism up to the light, and turning it in my small hand I could see in each turn a colour of the rainbow. I loved that prism and held it tightly so that I would not lose it; it became my Tardis (Time and Relative Dimensions in Space) (BBC TV, Dr Who, 2007) a womb, a heartbeat, container for my emotions. I felt everything was going to be all right.

The "character" of the accountancy profession: finding a prism

I use the prism as a metaphor for using the emotions within the accountancy profession to find what has been lost: ethical judgement, to tackle the dilemmas and paradoxes that are involved in money as energy, and loss of meaning when money is gambled and becomes separated from value and purpose. Using the Tardis to travel back in time, we can explore how the profession grew to its present institutional position and expose the split that has occurred that has made the management of money a "dirty" business that nobody seems to want to do.

Historical context

The modern accountancy profession grew out of the industrial revolution and the Protestant work ethic that "cleansed" the making of "profit': the bridge that made work, money, and profit palatable and morally acceptable (Weber, 2003) when there was unprecedented stability and prosperity in Europe (Pennington & Unwin, 2004). The "character" of the accountancy profession is a professional bureaucracy, developed from a psychological attitude emanating from Calvinism and the industrial revolution, a professional bourgeoisie that "held state, capitalism, religion, and profit-making" as a particularly Western European and American development (Weber, 2003). The new middle classes appear to have believed that they were the cohesive element in society, an antidote to autocracy, cruelty, and misery described in Dickensian London. They could solve all the ills of the world through philanthropic endeavour.

While the bourgeoisie grew out of a desire for cohesion, rather than revolution, with two world wars to show for it, the accountancy profession has not grown as one cohesive entity, and there have been various attempts at amalgamation over the past twenty years. The major accountancy professional bodies in the UK and Ireland joined together in 1974 to form the Consultative Committee of Accountancy Bodies (CCAB). CCAB is a limited company with six members: Institute of Chartered Accountants in England and Wales (ICAEW) (membership 126,000, students 10,000; 15,000+

ICAEW members working overseas); Institute of Chartered Accountants of Scotland (ICAS) (membership 15,000, trains around 800 students a year); Institute of Chartered Accountants in Ireland (ICAI); Association of Chartered Certified Accountants (ACCA) (the largest international professional accountancy body, with 320,000 members in 160 countries); Chartered Institute of Management Accountants (CIMA) (62,000 members and 81,000 students in 154 countries, 10 offices internationally, as well as headquarters in the UK); Chartered Institute of Public Finance and Accountancy (CIPFA) (the smallest UK based accountancy body—13,500 qualified members and 2,800 students). The Board of CCAB Ltd consists of six directors, senior members of the six member bodies. CCAB provides a forum in which matters affecting the profession as a whole can be discussed and co-ordinated and enables the profession to speak with a unified voice to government.

Although there is pressure for convergence in accounting standards world-wide, in the UK and Ireland the professional accounting bodies and their membership remain independent of each other. The profession is co-ordinated via a standardization of skills provided by standardized training, and there are dilemmas about how to deliver ethical training that requires a local context. To this day, the "character" of the accounting profession is bureaucratic, uncohesive, and maybe "misfit" for today's challenges; the profession might require change to an "interactive social character" (Maccoby, 1999).

The role of the accountant and accountancy profession is changing, and this materially affects what behaviours are required in order to get professional expertise listened to and acted upon: I am suggesting, here, that the accountancy bodies should take up their authority as ethical leaders in supporting and funding the development of ethical accountancy in the profession, and that this cannot be left to governments or any other institutions.

Primordial theories in use

The nineteenth and twentieth centuries reframed the way we understand ourselves as human beings. Charles Darwin (1809–1882) constructed a theory of natural selection that "placed man firmly in the animal kingdom" (Gay, 1989); Sigmund Freud (1856–1939) developed psychoanalysis into a general psychology, as the "predominate mode of discussing personality and interpersonal relationships" (Storr, 1989) and Albert Einstein's (1879–1955) theory of special relativity and general relativity, specifically mass energy equivalence $E = mc^2$, reframed our understanding of gravity, time, and space as a universal theory (Kilmister, 1971). In art, the emancipation of colour has had a primordial role, heightening feeling, compounding expectation, and representing a short cut to understanding (Russell, 1974). The same period saw the development of artistic freedom through movements that developed the independence of artists in "thought and aim" (Gaunt, 1970). We understand ourselves as individuals, in relation to groups, organizations, and society, global and universal.

Specific theories in use

I am focusing on the application of three specific theories that are meaningful to me in my consultancy practice and I believe are useful in helping the accountancy profession learn about itself and its external environment in order to deliver effective ethical training and leadership. These theories relate to boundaries, the use of sense data, and energy.

Bounded and unbounded systems

Themes from "boundary theory" (Miller & Rice, 1990) as applied to the accountancy profession as a system include its interdependent relationships, the regulation of transactions, the problem of overbounded systems unable to adapt quickly and effectively to changes and reverse the build up of entropy, physical and psychological boundaries. Working with psychological boundaries can tell more about the "here and now" of the system (Alderfer, 1980).

Alpha-function

Bion's (1962, p. 115) idea of an alpha-function to convert sense-data (in this approach, colour, observation, sight) into alpha elements to provide the psyche with material for dream thoughts, the capacity to wake up or go to sleep, to be conscious or unconscious.

I extend this theory by linking this alpha-function to energy activated by "colour", which I describe as the emotional content, or sentient need, to create, fill up, and make whole that moves the individual from a paranoid–schizoid to a depressive position. Under this framing idea, "energy" is the undertow that drives meaning and motivation in work and organizational life.

Focus Energy Balance Indicator (FEBI) instrument

I am a trained practitioner in the use of the FEBI (Whitelaw, 2006), developed in the USA. The FEBI identifies energy patterns for performance and balance: driver, visionary, organizer, and collaborator. These energy patterns run through every person's nervous system and show up as interlinked qualities of movement, feeling, thought, and behaviour. To this I add two related patterns to make them explicit: Challenger and Passive–aggressive. These two patterns are tied to group experience, and relate to cross-boundary energy and ambiguous energy.

Experience from "Energy" workshop

In June 2006 I had been working with other consultants on the design of a leadership conference on the theme of "collaboration", and research lead me to consider the use of drama and improvization learning, particularly working across organizational boundaries. Coaching and conversations with leaders that were suffering from "burn-out", particularly in the charity field, had suggested to me that effective leadership and energy go hand in-hand. When energy is used up, so is the leadership.

I discussed my experience with a consulting colleague who made similar observations regarding leaders who were very successful in their work, but unsuccessful in their home life. A common concern expressed was a feeling of emptiness and dissatisfaction. Some leaders observed that they did not know how they had got to the positions they held. They were unloved by their children, and wanted to change, but could not stop what they were doing. Committed to the accumulation of material wealth, they felt they were behaving as if they were a "machine".

In July 2006, I asked a consultant who had been a theatre director and had worked extensively in the creative field, a colleague AOC consultant, and a fitness and life coach if they would join me in discussions about designing a leadership programme that would address the feelings of burn-out. After initial meetings where we shared information about ourselves and the ways we work, including our consulting domains, we decided that the conference should be life-enhancing, simplicity, "energy", and that participants would need to "surrender" to be prepared to play. We did not want participants to feel foolish; we would need to provide a safe "container".

We reflected upon our own energies during this planning phase, and the frustrations felt from misunderstandings, conflicting approaches, and a tug-of-war between us. We identified a number of issues: getting participants to admit they need to recharge their batteries (I felt this); would it be commercial (how can we afford to develop this approach without backing)? We wanted to focus on learning (but we also want to make money), and not to be contained by old rules and formulas (but that is what sells). We needed some new structure, and the confidence, flexibility, and energy to create a new system that makes sense of complexity.

We identified three components for the workshop: nutrition, condition, and mission, leading to the following questions: what is your mission?; what is your current condition?; what is going on to affect that condition? In getting people to locate/articulate what their mission is, we would examine the areas identified in Figure 1.

Agreement

1. The programme should focus on nutrition, condition, mission with the theme of ENERGY.

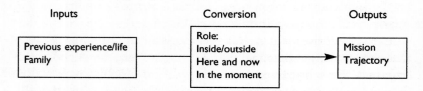

Figure 1.   The path to identifying one's mission.

2. Measures to evaluate before and after the event.
3. Energy to open up and experiment.
4. Using jazz , drama, and role play.

We agreed our mission was to re-energize leaders and be "the international leadership experience that re-connects people to their energy and power". We would work with participants to re-energize from the inside out, deconstruct/reconstruct, and be the "sunshine that melts the ice" by helping people to have the energy to "fall in love again"—to rediscover their "passion".

We used the image of a battery and a *personal energy management system* (PEM)—creating magnetic leadership: "We help people who lead to find the energy to do so".

Planned outcomes: by using PEMs we envisaged that participants will understand what personal energy is, where personal energy (PE) comes from, how to use PE to light up life and others, where to find the energy to start, the positive and negative applications of PE, where the energy leakages occur, how to re-charge their batteries, carry out an energy audit, build, manage, and maintain personal, team, and organization relationships, and the importance of energy elements and the roles of nutrition and condition in mission accomplishment.

There was significant enthusiasm about the concept, and to take the ideas we had discovered forward into experimentation. However, the momentum was lost due to the illness and death of a partner of one of the consultants, the birth of a baby for another of the consultants, and work commitments that took energies in other directions.

FEBI

Following this, in October 2006, I received a telephone call from an American company with offices in London, inviting me to participate in an international workshop where a new instrument called the Focus Energy Balance Indicator (FEBI) would be learnt. I attended the workshop, and was struck by the similarities to themes that had been explored elsewhere in terms of a scientifically tested system for locating personal and team energy patterns.

I became aware that the FEBI system had emanated from ballet. I had been involved in drawing and painting ballet dancers, which had alerted me to muscle tone, movement, and how energy is felt in the body. I had produced "flash art" sketches that located "energy" by matching colour to the strength of feeling and emotions conveyed in the muscle movement: the resistance, the force, power, sensuality. My observation was turned into application.

Leadership as performance: a planned pilot

In September 2007, I was hopeful of being able to pilot and test some of these ideas with the consultant in theatre in a workshop "Leadership as Performance", designed jointly with Birmingham University. However, the workshop had to be cancelled due to a lack of participants. During 2008 and the early part of 2009, I have taken these plans forward by using some of these ideas in coaching a client for the final selection board of the Civil Service fast stream, employing a group role play simulating collaborative decision making within a household of five young professionals about the allocation and use of scarce resources to address poverty and deprivation in a London Borough. Taking up their simulated roles as Advisers to, and representatives of, Ministers in a cross-departmental forum, participants were to both compete and collaborate in deciding the best use of resources.

From observing both body and verbal language within the group, I was able to detect the anxiety and political use of the simulation exercise that, underneath the surface, generated an unspoken debate about money within the household; thus, there were two debates going on: the role-play and the real-play in motion. This illuminated the challenge of being mindful of our role, identities, desires, and anxiety about ethical decision making and money, played out consciously and unconsciously across internal and external boundaries.

In May 2008, I had the opportunity to use both the Analytical Activity (p. 173) and Group Role Play (described above) in a residential workshop "Ethical leadership" with students studying for a Masters in Business Administration (MBA) and subsequently the Business Ethics Module, while coaching both part-time and full-time (mainly international) students. During this period, I worked with the drawn images created by students, and the associations for these in relation to ethical challenges headlined in the media. Students were tasked with identifying and exploring ethical challenges encountered and experienced in their own work and lives.

I have recently designed a one-day workshop with the Tavistock Institute entitled "The essential ethical leadership", which is currently being delivered (Spring 2009) and is aimed at the financial services sector at a time of global financial crisis and "Burn-out" in consumer spending.

Ways to work with accountants using creative media

Working with the theoretical frameworks outlined earlier, I am exploring a working hypothesis as described below.

An understanding of boundaries, whether organizational, personal, team, individual, or task, will help accountants focus their energy on the relatedness of their role, and develop self awareness. I link Darwin's "survival of the fittest", Einstein's theory of relativity, and Freud's psychology, through "energy" of the cosmos to Bion's alpha-function, to convert "sense data": our sense of place in magnetic relation to, and in competition with, the "other", the FEBI to our personal sensing of energy, in particular, what we feel, observe, and locate—motion, colour, and light.

If an appreciation of the role of energy as money and colour is a way of accessing judgement, then it is possible to develop a broader meaning of "value". If it is possible to change the "character" of the profession, then it will be possible to move accountancy from its current position to repair and provide reparation for past failures in perspective, and to learn from experience.

Self-knowledge is the "prism" of ethical leaders

Leaders need self-knowledge. "When white light is passed through a prism it is broken up into its constituent colours because different colours of light are bent through different angles in passing through the glass" (Kilmister, 1971). Judgements are often about seeing different angles that give different perspectives, and recognizing the different elements that go to making up a decision. I am suggesting that if leadership is combining task and sentience of varying brightness or luminosity to make ethical decisions, then ethical leadership depends on sensitivity to the intensity of experience or task (Russell, 1974).

A healthy leader is

> a circle (sphere) so that whatever is not-self can be described as inside or outside that person. It is not possible for persons to get further in society-building than they can get in their own personal development. [Winnicott, 1950, in Trist & Murray, 1990, pp. 546–557]

Without colour the circle

> is a sense of frame without a sense of picture, a sense of form without retention of spontaneity. This is a pro-society tendency that is anti-individual. People who develop in this way can be called "hidden anti-socials". [*ibid.*]

Ethical leadership: commitment to ethical behaviour

Objective: "Bring to life and engage students and professional accountants in the development of the accounting profession for ethical leadership".

Taking these ideas forward into planning for the development of ethical leadership, it will be important to use a range of activities involving consultation with the profession through to survey wider opinion and stakeholder views of what is required. It will be important to examine what other professional bodies (e.g., those for doctors, lawyers) do to develop ethical judgement. I envisage interventions that include the use of experiential learning (Kolb, 1984), action learning (Revans, 1998), managed play (Murray & Ostiund, 2001), story-telling (Salit, 2003), reflective practice (Pedler, Burgoyne, & Boydell, 2001) and coaching (Whitmore, 2001).

Activities would include drama, role-play to immerse participants in real-life situations, guest speakers, and practitioner participation, communicating ethical sensitivity, judgement and behaviour, and demonstrating ethical leadership. In role plays and simulations (Barker, 1977), a key issue would be to address how to

take ethical action in the face of dilemmas and paradoxes in organizations that challenge personal and professional ethics and
morals, and which might bring the individual into conflict with,
and possible harm from, work colleagues. Guest speakers would
need to be able to speak with authority from experience. Didactic
activities might include lectures on professional standards, discussions about democracy, capitalism, social change, surveillance, technology, value, and the environment.

A key issue is personal responsibility for developing self awareness through self-directed learning and continued professional
development: emotional development to understand theories of
behaviour; understanding and practising psychodynamics processes in groups; understanding body language, personal energy,
cultural differences, and boundary management; and the use of
judgement and self assessment of behaviours in contexts that challenge the normative use of principles, rules, and regulations.

The practice of designing interventions that work

I give here three examples of how art and media can be used to
engage students and professional accountants as primers to group
work, experiential learning through self review, and discussion by
(1) exploring ethics and the colour of money, (2) using energy and
art to explore ethics, and (3) using free association to derive meaning from boundaries without borders. Worked examples of materials are given below.

Example 1: Exploring ethics: the colour of money

The "colour of money" can be "green" (neutral) or a "dirty brown"
(excrement). Likewise, when running all colours together they
become a dirty brown. By looking through the prism of ethical
theory, which separates strands of colour, we can examine where
we stand in relation to ethical challenges.

Analytic Activity

Primer: There is something "dirty" about money and the language
we use to describe it: "Where there is muck there is money". "Dirty
money" is money that is illegally earned, illegally transferred, or

illegally utilized. If it breaks laws in its origin, movement, or use, then it qualifies for the label.

An ethical discourse about espoused ethical theory, and ethical theory in use, can help separate each colour to give clarity to our ethical stance and decision taking. Participants can identify their own theories in use to explore difference.

Discuss:
"What we have sown in the business of moving corrupt and commercial dirty money, we now reap in the inflow of criminal and terrorist money" (Baker, Dawson, Shulman, & Brewer, 2003, p. 2).

"For every $1 that is generously handed out in assistance across the top of the table, some $10 is taken back under the table" (Baker, Dawson, Shulman, & Brewer, 2003, p. 3).

Timothy 6:10 (King James Version)

"For the love of money is the root of all evil: which while some coveted after, they have erred from the faith, and pierced themselves through with many sorrows".

> PRIOR: . . . If He ever did come back, if He ever *dared* to show His face, or his Glyph or whatever in the Garden again . . . if after all this destruction, if after all the terrible days of this terrible century He returned to see . . . how much suffering His abandonment had created, if he did come back you should *sue* the bastard. That's my only contribution to all this Theology. Sue the bastard for walking out. How dare He.

> (*Pause*)

> ANGEL: Thus spake the prophet.

> [*Angels in America: Perestroika* Act 5, Kushner (1994), cited by Dubnick & Justice (2004, p. 3)]

Experience of using this analytic activity

I have used this analytical activity with MBA students in small groups, and in pairs, as part of an exploration of business ethics in a global environment. On each of three occasions with different groups, the discourse between students has illuminated uncomfortable complex feelings and frustrations, exacerbated by the problems of words and language to express and locate what is known and felt but cannot be explained.

On two occasions images were presented of the Earth, differentiated between rich and poor in northern and southern hemispheres. Other differences discussed were the availability and use of technologies, whether business can be expected to protect natural resources, their role in climate change, "survival of the fittest", the "bottom line" and the powers of government to regulate effectively, opposed to the power of multi-national companies to adhere to and undermine such regulation.

Example 2: Energy and art to explore ethics

Using the metaphor of a prism to develop sensitivity to personal energy location and deployment—what we see, what we know, what we estimate—extending the use of FEBI. Work with participants to paint their own energy "as felt" from different energy location, bringing together head, mind, and body: the physical action of painting "energy" can help make explicit an emotional awareness of ethical theories in use, the intuitive sensitivity of ethical assertions and judgement in situation and context. Identifying and using fragments of different ethical theories evolve over time into learned motor experience and movement, integrated through energy in the individual, group, and organization. Through the FEBI and art we can explore and reinforce our understanding of our emotions and ethical theory in relation to head, heart, and guts (Dotlich, Cairo, & Rhinesmith, 2006).

Example 3: Using free association to derive meaning

In the Beginning (see p. 175) has several general meanings. Painted on a wood palette, the paint as a memory within a tube, yet to be squeezed out, the palette (the masculine brown wood expectant attribution of light), the recognition of the sensual colour forms without lines (the emotional content, feelings), the beginning of a new creation (life and birth), the beginning of new horizons

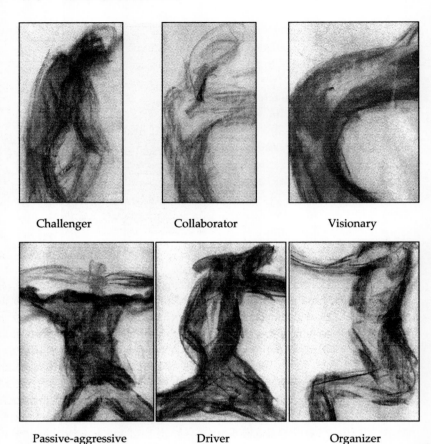

Challenger   Collaborator   Visionary

Passive-aggressive   Driver   Organizer

(recovery): an energetic "big bang" explosion, continuous, growing with no boundaries.

The oscillation between fragments and whole, and symbol formation through play as a discharge of mental energy linking mind and body in symbolic formation is a Kleinian theme (Hinshelwood, 1989) which was later taken up by Bion in describing the alpha-funtion and beta-function as mental energy (Bion, 1962a, cited in Hinshelwood, 1989) representing mechanisms which link all creative endeavours.

At the whole level, the painting captures "energy" within a frame. It is an open "window", but not empty. The white paint symbolizes an energy source (purity, perfection, and light), dark

In the Beginning (Kevin Dixon, 1997).

green, money (safety, prudence, hope), black, information technology (control, fear, black holes, surveillance), blue, accounting standards (rules, compliance, conservative, integrity, seriousness), and purple, governance (power, dependency, childhood) are some of the colour–symbols–emotions experienced. Moving from each emotion, the fragmentation is repaired as a living whole.

The universe, the Earth, the self, is a sphere that is not a prison: use "free association" to access self knowledge as a source of energy for linking the tangible and intangible, reality and dreams, for discussions about identity, roles, and professional boundaries.

Conclusions and recommendations

This chapter brings together the identified need for ethical education in the accountancy profession of which I am a member, and my learning as a consultant in private practice. The accountancy profession has identified a need for the development of ethical training. I believe the focus should be providing accountants with the skills to become ethical leaders. Ethical leaders have to have good judgement that can be developed in the classroom as well as in the field. The profession needs to shift from an over-dependency on rules and principles to the development, maturation, and growth of accountants who have ethical standards integral to learning.

Public confidence in the profession requires the profession to learn. Understanding resistance to learning is a way of unlocking and "working through" ethical issues to design ethical training with the purpose of providing integrated learning opportunities for accounting professionals to explore psychological challenges of ethical leadership, to energize students and qualified accounting professionals by using self-reflection, and to facilitate understanding and working through emotional resistance.

I am recommending that the challenges identified by the profession can be met by a strategy that involves accountants and restores public confidence in the profession. I am suggesting here that providing the participant with the knowledge, sensitivity, judgement, and behaviours to navigate ethical challenges requires "here and now" experiential learning. I would like there to be a debate about ethical leadership in the boardroom, in the profession. I would like the professional bodies to provide funding to experiment with the possibility of designing ethical learning opportunities for accountants using art, drama, improvisation and story-telling, whereby individuals develop their own powers of judgement about moral dilemmas in work.

Note

1. This paper is a registered activity as part of "Refreshing the Tavistock Institute's intellectual traditions".

References and bibliography

Alderfer, C. (1980). Consulting to underbounded systems. In: C. P. Alderfer & C. L. Cooper (Eds.), *Advances in Experiential Social Processes, Volume 2* (pp. 267–295). New York: Wiley.

Argyris, C., & Schön, D. A. (1974). *Theory in Practice: Increasing Professional Effectiveness*. San Francisco, CA: Jossey-Bass.

Baker, R., Dawson, B., Shulman, I., & Brewer, C. (2003). *Dirty Money and its Global Effects*. International Policy Report, Centre for International Policy.

Barker, C. (1977). *Theatre Games*. London: Methuen.

Bion, W. (1962). *Learning from Experience*. London: Heinemann.

Consultative Committee of Accountancy Bodies (CCAB) (2006). *CCAB Ethics Education Forum Event Report*, December. Available at: www.ccab.org.uk/PDFs/EventEducationReport.pdf

Dixon, K. (2004). Factors that help and hinder changes to operations in the public service in UK and Ireland. MA Dissertation, Tavistock Institute.

Dotlich, D. L., Cairo, P. C., & Rhinesmith, S. H. (2006). *Head, Heart, and Guts: How the World's Best Companies Develop Complete Leaders*. San Francisco, CA: Wiley.

Dr Who (2007). *Tardis*, BBC Television Series, London.

Dubnick, M. J., & Justice, J. B. (2003). *The Evil of Administrative Ethics*. Working Paper QU/GOV/9/2004, Institute of Governance Public Policy and Social Research (p. 3). Queens University, Belfast.

Financial Reporting Council Professional Oversight Board (2008). *Key Facts and Trends in the Accountancy Profession*. London: FRC

Gaunt, W. (1970). *The Impressionists*. London: Thames & Hudson.

Gay, P. (1989). *Freud. A Life for our Time*. New York: Anchor.

Global Witness (2007). *Oil Revenue Transparency: A Strategic Component of US Energy Security and Anti-Corruption Policy*. Washington: Global Witness Publishing Corporation.

Hake, E. R. (2005). Financial illusion: accounting for profits in an Enron world. *Journal of Economic Issues*, 39: 1. Questia: http://www.questia.com/read

Harman, G. (1997) *The Nature of Morality: an Introduction to Ethics*. New York: Oxford University Press.

Hinshelwood, R. D. (1989). *A Dictionary of Kleinian Thought*. London: Free Association.

International Education Practice Statement 1 (IEPS 1) (2006). *Approaches to Developing and Maintaining Professional Values, Ethics and Attitude*. www.ifac.org/store (free download).

International Federation of Accountants (IFAC) (2007). *Strategic and Operational Plan 2008–2009*. www.ifac.org/store (free download).

Kellerman, B. (2004). *Bad Leadership*. Boston, MA: Harvard Business School Press.

Kilmister, C. (1971). *The Nature of the Universe*. London: Thames & Hudson.

Knight, R., & Knight, M. (1951). *A Modern Introduction to Psychology*. London: University Tutorial Press Ltd.

Kolb, D. (1984). *Experiential Learning: Experience as the Source of Learning and Development*. Englewood Cliffs, NJ: Prentice-Hall.

Maccoby, M. (1999). The self in transition: from bureaucratic to inter-active social character. Paper presented to the American Academy of Psychoanalysis, 43rd Annual Meeting, 14 May.

Miller, E. J., & Rice A. K. (1990). *Task and Sentient Systems and their Boundary Controls, the Social Engagement of Social Science, Vol. 1.* London: Free Association.

Mukherjee, J. K. (2003). *The Practice of the Integral Yoga.* Pondicherry, India: Sri Aurobindo Ashram Press.

Murray, S., & Ostiund, A. (2001). *Managing Play: A Master Thesis in Entrepreneurship.* Stockholm: Stockholm School of Economics.

Pedler, M., Burgoyne, J., & Boydell, T. (2001). *A Managers Guide to Self-Development* (4th edn). London: McGraw-Hill.

Pennington, M., & Unwin, S. (2004). *A Pocket Guide to Ibsen, Checkhov and Strindberg.* London: Faber and Faber.

Raines, J. P., & Leathers, C. G. (1996). Veblenian stock markets and the efficient markets hypothesis. *Journal of Post Keynesian Economics, 19*(1): 137–152.

Revans, R. W. (1998). *ABC of Action Learning: Empowering Managers to Act and Learn from Action.* London: Lemos & Crane.

Russell, J. (1974). *The Emancipation of Colour, Volume 2.* New York: Museum of Modern Art.

Salit, C. R. (2003). The coach as theatre director. *Journal of Excellence, 8:* 40.

Storr, A. (1989). *Freud.* Oxford: Oxford University Press.

Weber, M. (2003) [1904–1905]. *The Protestant Ethic and the Spirit of Capitalism* T. Parsons (Trans.). New York: Dover.

Whitelaw, G. (2006). *Focus Energy Balance Indicator.* USA: Mercer Delta.

Whitmore, J. (2001). *Coaching for Performance.* London: Nicholas Brealey.

Winnicott, D. W. (1950). Thoughts on the meaning of the word democracy. In: E. Trist & H. Murray (1990) *The Social Engagement of Social Science, a Tavistock Anthology Volume 1. The Socio-Pyschological Perspective* (pp 546–557). London: Free Association Books.

CHAPTER TEN

The use of history in organizational consultancy interventions

Antonio Sama

Introduction

This chapter, drawing data from a long-term consultancy (ten years) that the author is involved with, analyses the place history (as collection of stories) has in the life cycle of value-led organizations. It will engage with the issue of if, and how much, an organization's future is locked in by historical events and how consultant and client can work with it. It also discusses how organizational consultancy can become a more history-orientated discipline. It is argued that including history in the consultants' domains can contribute to increasing choices in actionable knowledge for the mindful consultant.

The chapter refers to a case of an Italian social enterprise for whom thinking and planning for the future has meant addressing the past.

The case

Social enterprise and social firm

The consultancy started with "scouting" on the move. Anna (in order to protect confidentiality the names of the representative of the client system and the name of the client system have been changed), the representative of the client system, and the consultant had the first conversation while travelling together by car. Anna was, at the time, the manager of Flamenco, one of the service delivery units of Galaxy (the client system).

Galaxy is a large voluntary organization with several subsystems providing social and health care and employment for disadvantaged people through the business models of the social enterprise and social firm. In 1998, Galaxy had seventeen members (six men and eleven women) and ran two health and social care service provider units, two production units (with the business model of co-operative). Its members were also involved in running—as volunteers—self-help and voluntary groups as well as taking part in public campaigns.

When Anna met the consultant she was temporarily asked (by the leading people in the organization) to take up a general organizational role as—although not formalized—the managing director of Galaxy. This request came about because Galaxy was facing a survival crisis brought about by the incompetence and malpractice of the employed accountant. The overt organizational issue was described by Anna as a general feeling (intuition) of something not right in the organization, a feeling of discomfort widely spread.

The organizational model known as "social enterprise" includes development trusts, co-operatives, credit unions, and community business. A social enterprise is a business that trades for a social purpose. The "social firm" is a "market led" enterprise set up specifically to create employment for people severely disadvantaged in the labour market. (These definitions have been agreed by Social Firms UK; they can be found at http://www.socialfirms.co.uk/index.php/Section99.html.) Thus, a "social firm" could be described as a sub-system of the larger system "social enterprise". It is part of the Third Sector that incorporates voluntary and community sector organizations and social enterprise.

Social firms are businesses that combine a market orientation and a social mission ("businesses that support" rather than "projects that trade"). They are workplaces where the working environment is one that provides all employees with support, opportunity, and meaningful work. Social firms are committed to the social and economic integration of disadvantaged people through employ-ment. A key means to this end is economic empowerment through the payment of market wages to all employees.

Usually, social firms emerge in local markets where there is no need of large investments, and very often because there are charis-matic leaders. Managerial skills and processes are very often learnt on the job and through trial and error. Essential to the success of a social enterprise or social firm are links with the local community and the amount of social capital the organization can muster (Grove, 1997; Munday & Sama, 2000). (There are currently 137 busi-nesses in the Social Firm sector in the UK; an increase of 15% over 2005. Sixty-seven of these 137 businesses are fully fledged Social Firms; this is an increase in the number of Social Firms of 37% over 2005. The Social Firm sector has created a total of 1,652 full time equivalent jobs; 861 of these FTE jobs [52%] are held by severely disadvantaged people—primarily people with disabilities. An aver-age of 841 trainees benefit from placements in the Social Firm sector each week; fifty-seven individuals moved into employment posi-tions outside the Social Firm sector during 2006–2007 [http://resources.socialfirms.co.uk/resourcefiles/2006-7%20Mapping%20Brochure.pdf].)

The intervention

The entering and contracting stage took five months (from November 1997 to March 1998). In this period, the consultant met once more with the representative and twice with the representa-tive and the President of the client system. (This couple can be described as the top management.) Following these meetings, a working note (Miller, 1995) was produced, discussed, and agreed with the top management of the organization. The working note spelt out the themes and issues discussed, a first description of the organization and its issues as described by the top management, and a proposal for intervention. It was agreed that, rather than intervening in one of the sub-systems or addressing one cluster of the many issues, the intervention should involve the whole system.

The note identified that alongside the formal Management Board (made up of five people) Galaxy was, effectively, run and managed by a shadow system. (Shadow system is described by Stacey [1996, p. 290] as

> the set of interactions among members of a legitimate organizational system that fall outside that legitimate system. It comprises social and political interactions that are outside the rules strictly prescribed by the legitimate system. It is the arena in which members of an organization pursue their own gain, but also the arena in which they play, create and prepare innovations.

Mintzberg [1991] calls this the "political" form of organizations, driven by the force of competition.) It was suggested that a data gathering and feedback seminar was necessary before planning any further intervention.

At this stage, it was helpful to hold in mind the differences between research and data-driven inquiry on the one hand, and client-driven inquiry on the other. Schein (1995) advocates the need to consider data gathering not just as the preliminary collection of information, but also as an OD intervention. As he put it more bluntly,

> if we take a clinical perspective, we must assume that the way in which we enter a diagnostic relationship with a client is in itself a major intervention that must be evaluated as an intervention, not just as a method of gathering information. Or, to put it more concretely, we start intervening when we first pick up the phone and answer an inquiry from a potential client. [*ibid.*, p. 14]

The approach (data-driven or client-driven) will determine whose needs are met. Schein, starting from an action research perspective, distinguishes between the researcher's agenda (data-driven approach) to which the client is associated, and the client's agenda (client-driven) with which the researcher is involved.

Following the seminar, agreement was reached with the top management on:

- a working hypothesis that Galaxy was engaged in establishing a new balance between its past and its future by interrogating the current meaning of the organization's original values;
- the identification of the members of the organization to be involved in the next stage (these were identified as the managers of the subsystems and the major opinion leaders);

- the consultant's access to the organization's archive, to the identified members, and to the sub-systems.

Further data gathering activities lasted five months. These activities included:

- analysis of all relevant documentation produced by the client system in its twenty-one years of existence;
- analysis of the budget of the past two financial years;
- observation visits lasting at least one day in three main subsystems;
- face-to-face interviews with nine middle managers and opinion leaders.

Data were sought on the following:

- the organization's primary task (Rice, 1963 defines the "primary task" of an organization as the task a system or any of its parts has to perform in order to survive) as understood by the members;
- the organization's history and its strengths and its weakness;
- processes for job and task allocation;
- the organizational internal climate, both in subsystems and in the organization as a whole;
- the decision making processes;
- the organization's policies and practices around human resources (e.g., recruitment, professional development, reward systems, etc.);
- prevailing models of development and change to address challenges facing the organization now and in the future.

Interviews were designed having in mind the agreement achieved with the top management. As Schein (1995) put it

> The consultant must raise the question of what would be the consequence of interviewing the subordinates or doing the survey, of how the data would be fed back and what kinds of confidentiality would be guaranteed. Of greatest importance at this stage is also to share with the contact client the possible outcomes, especially the possibility that the data will reveal a problem in the relationship of

the client to the people who will be interviewed or surveyed. In other words, what if a lot of negative data come out about the boss who is launching the project? Is he or she ready for it? How will they handle the feedback? [p. 16]

The interviews produced thirteen hours of recorded material. The final working hypothesis was that the organization was a family-like social enterprise struggling to manage the boundaries between the business and the family sides.

The report produced was presented and discussed in a first meeting with the top management and few days later to the whole organization; this included all members. As result of the feedback seminar and the discussion that followed, the top management and the middle managers (with the agreement of the opinion leaders) asked for a second consultancy intervention looking at a new organizational and job design. A new management structure and, consequently, a new management board were seen as the final result of the second stage of the consultancy. The consultant was asked to support the top management and the new management board in the transition process.

Institutionalization

The transition process took over a year. As a result, the organization was divided into four sub-systems: voluntary organization, social enterprise, finance, and training. The voluntary organization maintained the original name and would be engaged in leading and taking part in political and social campaigns aimed at promoting the values the original organization stood for (e.g., human rights, equal opportunities, legality, fair trade, etc.). The social enterprise took up a new name (meaning the coming together of several streams) and would include all the sub-systems involved in delivering contracted out social and health care and one social firm. Two sub-systems would serve the organization as a whole: finance and training (Figures 1(a, b) and 2). Following the institutionalization of the new design, the consultant was engaged in supporting individual managers (including Anna, who originally felt the need for a consultancy) through role consultation.

The new design was stable for over five years. Recently, the

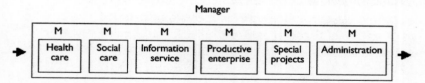

Figure 1(a). Galaxy organization at the start of the consultancy (original real). M = Manager.

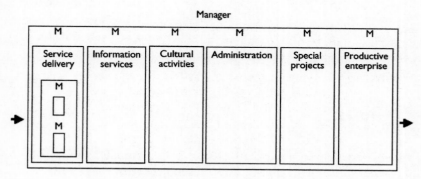

Figure 1(b). Galaxy (ideal) organization after consultancy (the organizational design intervention—the transitional). M = Manager.

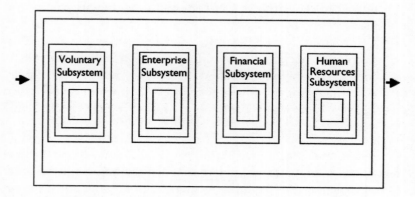

Figure 2. Galaxy actual organization (today real).

consultant has been approached for a follow-up intervention in order to check where the social enterprise is. At the same time, the original contact client has been appointed Managing Director of Galaxy, the first woman to achieve this.

The consultant–client relationship

Through the two stages of the consultancy, the consultant, as Schein stated, was involved in the issues Galaxy was facing. He becomes an agent, an accomplice (etymologically, "accomplice" means a confederate, a partner. It comes from the Latin *complicare*, "fold together"), and involved in the processes entrusted to construct new history, to move Galaxy from the present to the future (from the "real" [the "here", the present, the constraints and issues] to the "ideal" [the "then", the future, the change] [Dartington, Miller, & Gwynne, 1981]). The consultant's reflective practice about the past had three main areas to work with.

1. The description—made by client system—of Galaxy's history as well as its history with "methods and techniques for organizational change and development which they want to continue or alter in some way" (Neumann, 2004, p. 15). (It could be described as learning about the client and, in doing so, being in the "here and now" of the consultancy.)

2. The impact of this description on the consultant's recollection of the history of the sector and the social, economical, and cultural environment/context he was consulting in. (It could be described as learning about the industry and its trends and modification over time.)

3. The redefinition of the history of his professional identity, development, and practice. It is the history before entering consultancy. In this case, it was a previous professional identity as a trainer for social care practitioners. (It could be described as learning about and developing the consultant's professional domain and practice.)

Reflection on one's practice (Schön, 1983) of professional competences has been described as a crucial activity and ability in order to hold together the consultant's identity in a boundaryless occupation. The framework of reflective practice is secured by what Weick calls "milestones in competence" (Weick, 2001, p. 208).

The transition from milestone to milestone is the history (the story-making) of a consultant's professional identity and development, and its description (found, for example, in consultants' marketing material) is the consultant's historical narrative (the story-telling). It is through story-telling that the consultant describes what Neumann (2004, p. 16) calls "incremental adjustments to the foreground and background elements of their domain".

Such story-making is made of "painful breaks" in the relatedness between the consultant and his/her career, the painful breaks shaping a new professional identity.

It is similar to that which organizations experience at times, when being thrown out of equilibrium and losing their identity and relatedness to their environment.

Looking back, was this consultant aware of these processes going on? Not completely. Was it possible for him, reasonably, to be more aware than he was? Not really.

As Fuller (1995, p. 121), quoted by Booth (2003), put it

> Events happen in bundles, and only after some time has passed are they unravelled and labelled. This is the stuff of which historical narratives are made. And only through such retellings of the past do we come to have any strong sense of what the world obliges, forbids, or merely permits.

Understanding how these reflective processes can become part of the consultant's awareness is the main contribution of this case to my professional development.

The full extent of the learning came to light from re-engaging with the Galaxy experience some years later. For me, and for many consultants, there are cases and/or clients that are founding experiences in shaping our identities and professional domains. There are also certain frames of reference that are formative in configuring individual professional practices.

The theory: the frame of reference

The relation between history and organizations can be traced back to the work of the American scholar Alfred Chandler (1977). His recollection of the rise of the large corporations is regarded as the major historical work on organizations. Among the limitations, critics point to the deterministic nature of historical evolution as described by Chandler (Marens, 2005).

With Chandler, we are still in the paradigm of the grand narrative to understand large and long-lasting human and societal process. A consultant attempting to introduce history in organizational consultancy through this "door" inevitably risks introducing the limitations and the pitfalls of any grand narrative in trying to understand complex—and very often fragmented—processes.

Another way to utilize a historical perspective is to use history as the "mother-discipline", both to analyse organizations (Booth, 2003) and to understand the history of particular forms of organization (e.g., the formal organization, as in Dwyer, 2005). This approach recognizes that the concept of "path dependency" is useful and needed in order to understand how organizations operate and develop. It is described as a concept useful for researchers as well as managers.

Path dependency—from the discipline of economics—implies that the future of an organization is not infinite in its possibilities; on the contrary, it is limited by the choices made in the past. Organizations, through present decisions, close down some potential choices about the future. And these choices that constrain and limit the possibilities of future actions are not only the most visible ones, but also the small and almost invisible ones. Such choices will then form what is called "repertoires of routines" (*ibid*, p. 96) that the consultancy has to address and work with.

However, all these approaches are very limited in terms of offering useful advice for organizational consultancy practice. To use history to inform intervention design, the focus of attention needs to move from sense-making through macro histories (grand narratives and general theories) to sense-making through micro histories.

Over an organization's life cycle, individuals and groups subjectively define and interpret their environments, both internal and external. An organizational consultant and his/her client system can work for planned organizational change by using the historical narratives constructed over time and embedded in artefacts such as stories and symbols, etc. The concept of the symbolic artefact "belongs" to the cultural perspective on organizations, particularly to the concept of situated knowledge and community of practice (Gherardi, 2000; Wenger, 2000). In this perspective, artefacts are documents, tools, stories, symbols, etc., used by a community of practice (in this case the members of an organization) to maintain and develop itself. These can provide data for working on the organizational question(s) the consultancy is asked to address and for planning the organizational intervention(s).

History, as a collection of micro and meta narratives, also institutionalizes the description of how learning has taken place. In other words history is—alongside the actual archive—the repository of "how we learn(ed) to do things here".

In becoming history, narratives become reified, explaining why things have happened, or why they cannot happen in the future, because of the past. In this way, histories can serve to protect members of an organization from anxieties, from embarrassment and unfinished business, and also from learning. History can be evoked by client and consultant as the justification for the *status quo*, for not changing.

I describe this consultancy as a move from "story-telling" towards "story-making" (Johansson, 2004). As Galaxy was stuck in retelling the same stories about its development and it identity, so was I in relation to my professional identity and my domain. Only a joint move from story-telling to story-making would have made the consultancy effective and make accessible to me the full learning of a professional development programme I attended just before the start of the consultancy. As Johansson states, it means moving from "merely tell[ing] a story retrospectively about experience" to "living out experience in narrative forms . . . the consultancy process can be seen metaphorically as the construction of a plot to be enacted by the client and the consultant" (p. 341). Both Galaxy and I had to deal with what had happened over time. We had to acknowledge that retelling the usual stories will take us nowhere, and that acknowledgement was necessary to regain authority towards our story.

The transition from story-telling to story-making is a necessary part of the consultancy; it cannot be avoided. In order to have organizational change, a reference point is needed. It is against this point that differences can be planned/seen/experienced, and the reference point is the past. It is the relation to the past that the consultancy needs to change in order to shape the future. However, as Ooi (2002, p. 606) demonstrates, the past "is subjected to misrepresentation, mis-recollection and manipulation".

To work with the past, particularly in human services organizations where values play an important role, it is useful to identify those founding myths (Bartlett & Ghoshal, 1989; Child, 1987; Kimberly & Bouchikhi, 1995; Schein, 2004) that mobilize energy at the start-up stage and at critical moments in the life cycle of the organization. Such myths, overtime, can work against organizational change. The presenting task in this consultancy became to interrogate the founding myths, "unpack" them, and "repack" new ones, safely. In doing so, it might be expected that strong emotions in the client system and in the consultant are mobilized (Ooi, 2002, pp. 618–619).

Galaxy founding myths

At the founding of value-led organizations, a crucial role is played by first leaders, who give shape to the original organizational design, the construction of the internal integration processes, and how the organization relates to its environment. As such, organizational histories are the retelling of those

> shared basic assumptions that was learned by a group as it solved its problems of external adaptation and internal integration, that has worked well enough to be considered valid and, therefore, to be taught to new members as the correct way you perceive, think, and feel in relation to those problems. [Schein, 2004, p. 17]

Galaxy's founding myth—as gathered from the interviews and the various micro narratives—can be summarized as follows:

1. "We can show that it is possible to live together in innovative ways because we are the local "branch" of a larger national experience that did it before us."
2. "We come together from different experience and we choose to be together. This makes us a cohesive group."
3. "Our internal environment and experience makes it possible to overcome differences."
4. "The difficulties and struggles of the first years of our history show that we can survive and thrive against all odds."

The organizational implications of these myths (key narratives— cultural facts as Schein would define them) that supported the early development of Galaxy were identified as follows:

1. "Living together", being the organization's mission, was the primary task; anything else was contingent and instrumental to the held value. If in doubt, any activity that apparently threatened the mission was abandoned.
2. New members were assessed over a probation period, and only after such time would become full members. This was coherent with the voluntary organization, but became a burden when Galaxy needed to appoint new members of staff for the subsystem delivering health and social care.
3. Whoever has an idea for a new activity, once it received approval, will be in charge of making it happen, without any specific role or reward.
4. Galaxy is independent of the local constraints and will look for opportunity outside the local community and the local economics and political dynamics.

These cultural facts sustained Galaxy in its development for over two decades. The success of the first consultancy episode was that it allowed them to be changed. Currently, there are new stories being told; these new stories are also the accounts of the story-making that was the consultancy. For example, among the new stories has emerged that:

● our mission finds space and meaning also in activities/ventures that seem distant from our original idea;
● we need to select the best people for the job and there are professionals who do not share all our values but who are close to them and who can contribute to what we do;
● some of us are more suited for some activities than others, and we can differentiate among us, allocating formal responsibilities and giving job titles that include the words "responsible" or "manager".

The professional practice: how to work with history

Story-making as professional practice draws on the consultant's recollection of historical data, both as emotional memories and as embedded in reports, working notes, articles, etc. It was in going back to the professional development programme mentioned before that the consultant was able to move his identity from story-telling to story-making. It was the acknowledgement that a "painful break" had happened that helped the consultant's story-telling to become unstuck. A first scientific account of that programme has been recently described (Neumann, 2007).

In order to re-engage with Galaxy, the consultant explored—through literature review, conversations with more experienced consultants and peer review—the following sense-making perspectives:

- organization as acting out an idea;
- drawing on history of ideas studies (philological attention to particulars and details, to trends, to differences, and to similarities);
- understanding the values in relation to the context (mapping its societal, cultural, and political stands in relation to the context);
- mapping the organization in relation to the national and local debate;
- mapping the organization and its values in relation to the trends in European voluntary organization and reforms of the welfare state (map its ethical and political position).

All this work and these activities were felt to be a way to come closer to the client system. How did the perspectives above make sense from a consulting perspective? What extra did they offer? The outcome was an increased consultant's "psychological presence". Only when the consultant (re)gained a higher degree of psychological presence in relation to the client system and its history was he able to work towards the requested increasing of the degree of the psychological presence in the client system and between the client system and its environment (Kahn, 1992, p. 322). In order to be fully present in the client system, I had to rework my own sense of self in my past roles with this client; this had been a way to avoid the work in the present by turning the face towards the past.

I invited Galaxy's members to look at their collective past and to identify the elements of the founding myths and translate them not into activities, but into a new organization design. In order to do so, I worked with the new top management. It was crucial to create a holding environment in which Galaxy members would feel safe in reworking the founding myths. The actual activities became instrumental: a sort of container that allowed that particular content (rework the past) to take place without threatening the existence of Galaxy. This work was carried out in four interventions.

1. An organizational analysis exploring how the funding myths were embedded in the practice of each sub-system carried out by a manager of another of Galaxy's sub-systems.
2. An educational event on what the role and responsibilities of a top manager in Galaxy would be in order to address the way roles and responsibilities were allocated in the past and how they should be reworked to face the new design.
3. A series of sessions of process consultation with the new management board in order to identify and to support the changing way of carrying out business.
4. Role consultation to Anna (and to other managers) in order to support individuals in addressing the implications, at individual level (and at the level of individual story-making), of the changes.

The argument of this chapter is that what has been described above *is* working with history in organizational consultancy. The process seems well known, the intervention technology is unchanged, what is different is the sense-making perspective used.

Indications for consulting practice

Reflecting on the consultation to Galaxy can provide some generalization about the use of history in organizational consultancy. They can be summarized as listed below.

1. Considering an organization as the practical implementation of an idea and not just a functional structure (Dartington, 1998) allows the consultant to look, from the start of the consultancy, at the symbolic and sense-making nature of the client organization, its processes as well as the organizational problem presented. From this standpoint, organizational history is the story of how that idea and its implementation have/have not

worked. This understanding of aims and origins provides a less politicized way of engaging with planned change than an audit or evaluative way of thinking. It allows the client (and consultant) to embrace the past and to include it in the change process rather than being judged and cut off (as sometimes, for example, interventions aimed at re-engineering the organizations seem to advocate).

2. History is a collection of stories, including the consultant's. For an organization to leave its past and find a new identity and sense of purpose, the consultant may have to do the same. History helps in tracing how one's identity (both consultant and client system) has been formed, and which "painful breaks" have contributed to shaping it. A consultant who has "worked" with and through his/her history can address this in respect of the clients. It is like being able to promote and support systemic change if one has experienced change in his/her own personal experience/life. A consultant who has worked with history in his/her practice is also aware of how environmental forces (like industry trends) in the past have contributed in shaping the organizational issues of the present.

3. Stories are symbolic artefacts to which we are attached. They give us a sense of familiarity, continuity, and security. We can always find the way "home" by listening to and telling stories: professional and organizational belonging are immediately recognizable from the stories told and listened to. Stories are the first way newcomers are socialized into a new organization or a new profession. This happens before any formal and structured induction. Abandoning them can be very painful; it is like entering new and unknown territories. It is important to avoid leaving the client, and the consultant, without stories to tell. Future work, institutionalizing new stories, is an essential aspect of working with the past.

4. The use of history in consultancy practice offers rich and contested data for diagnosing organizational issues and institutionalizing change. These are the data that sustain or frustrate motivation, energy and organizational commitment. Using history allows the activity of "probing" the client system, and the consultant, deep into the origin of the organizational issue or the professional identity that surface. This allows the insti-

tutionalization of change to be strongly secured, and to survive and serve the client system (and the consultant) for a long time.

References

Bartlett, C. A., & Ghoshal, S. (1989). *Managing Across Borders: The Transnational Solution*. London: Hutchinson.

Booth, C. (2003). Does history matter in strategy? The possibilities and problems of counterfactual analysis. *Management Decision, 41*: 96–104.

Chandler, A. (1977). *The Visible Hand: Managerial Revolution in American Business*. Cambridge, MA: Belknap.

Child, J. (1987). Managerial strategies, new technology and the labor process. In: J. M. Pennings & A. Buitendam (Eds.), *New Technology as Organizational Innovation*. Cambridge, MA: Ballinger.

Dartington, T. (1998). From altruism to action: primary task and the not-for-profit organization. *Human Relations, 51*: 1477–1493.

Dartington, T., Miller, E., & Gwynne, G. (1981). *A Life Together. An Exploratory Study of the Distribution of Attitudes around the Disabled*. London: Tavistock.

Dwyer, R. J. (2005). Formal organizations in contemporary society. The relevance of historical perspectives. *Management Decision, 43*: 1232–1248.

Fuller, S. (1995). A tale of two cultures and other higher superstitions. *History of the Human Science, 8*, 115–125.

Gherardi, S. (2000). Practice-based theorizing on learning and knowing in organizations. *Organization, 7*: 211–223.

Grove, B. (1997). *Social Firm Handbook: New Directions in the Employment, Rehabilitation and Reintegration of People with Mental Health Problems*. Brighton: Pavilion Publishing.

Johansson, A. W. (2004). Consulting as story-making. *Journal of Management Development, 23*: 339–354.

Kahn, W. A. (1992). To be fully there: psychological presence at work. *Human Relations, 45*: 321–349.

Kimberly, J. R., & Bouchikhi, H. (1995). The dynamics of organizational development and change: how the past shapes the present and constrains the future. *Organization Science, 6*: 9–18.

Marens, R. (2005). Getting it right the first time. Alfred Chandler, anthracite coal, and the origins of the American management. *Management Decision, 43*, 433–449.

Miller, E. (1995). Dialogue with the client system: use of the "working note" in organizational consultancy. *Journal of Managerial Psychology, 10*: 27–30.

Mintzberg, H. (1991). The Effective Organization: Forces and Forms. *Sloan Management Review, 32*: 54–67.

Munday, B., & Sama A. (Eds.) (2000). *From Welfare to Enterprise. Lessons from the ARTO Third System and Employment Project.* Canterbury: EISS.

Neumann, J. E. (2004). Reforming consultancy identity in relation to discontinuities with clients. Paper presented to the Academy of Management Annual Meeting, New Orleans.

Neumann, J. E. (2007). Becoming better consultants through varieties of experiential learning. In: M. Reynolds & R. Vince (Eds.), *The Handbook of Experiential Learning in Management Education* (pp. 258–273). Oxford: Oxford University Press.

Ooi, C. (2002). Persuasive histories. Decentring, recentring and emotional crafting of the past. *Journal of Organizational Change, 15*: 606–621.

Rice, A. K. (1963). *The Enterprise and Its Environment: A System Theory of Management.* London: Tavistock.

Schein, E. H. (1995). Process consultation, action research and clinical inquiry: are they the same? *Journal of Managerial Psychology, 10*: 14–19.

Schein, E. H. (2004). *Organizational Culture and Leadership.* San Francisco, CA: Jossey-Bass.

Schön, D. A. (1983). *The Reflective Practitioner. How Professionals Think in Action.* New York: Basic Books.

Stacey, R. (1996). *Complexity and Creativity in Organizations.* San Francisco, CA: Berrett-Koehler.

Weick, K. E. (2001). *Making Sense of the Organization.* Boston, MA: Blackwell.

Wenger, E. (2000). Communities of practice and social learning systems. *Organization, 7*: 225–246.

Endnote. Mind-fulness as meta- and micro-narratives: the encouragement to mind-fulness offered by working with narrative structure

Karen Izod

These chapters are the tales from the field as told by thirteen members of the AOC society, who, together with their associates, wanted to write about their consulting experiences and bring them to a wider readership. Coming from different professional backgrounds, nationalities, and perspectives, they found themselves being challenged by who they were and how they were perceived in their stories. They told of how they inhabited, responded to, and shaped their stories with the organizational characters, issues, and contexts they met along the way. They brought their stories to some kind of ending, and spoke to us, as readers, regarding what we might think about those endings. These are the narratives that authors have used to relate their experiences and their thinking.

This ending note attempts to address mind-fulness as a continuing engagement with micro-narratives, and to explore what consulting from this perspective means for individual practitioners and their clients. In response to the challenge set out in the introduction to this volume, that "mindfulness is a skill that can be cultivated by anyone" (Germer, 2005, p. 5), it suggests that narrative can be utilized as a means of being present in encounters that hold a potential for change and as a motif through which practitioners can develop their capacities for mind-fulness. Finally, it encourages readers to develop their own narratives about their consulting and operational practices, to counter circumstances in which they and their clients might self-limit their capacities to effect change, and to enhance possibilities for more playful, creative, and developmental encounters.

Revisiting mind-fulness

I am struck, in reading through these chapters, by how often the notion of mind-fulness has emerged from situations where something has got stuck. This might be in a problematic relationship between consultants attempting to work collaboratively (Walsh & Whittle), or in a client system that, together with the consultant, is struggling to find new positions to explore existing issues (Van Linge), or in the thinking and behaviours of the consultant, acknowledging that some kind of shift in perspective is needed (Sama). Being mind-ful, with its emphasis on intentionality and choice, paradoxically comes into being most especially when options feel limited and pathways are unclear.

So, is this capacity to engage in a mind-ful stance under these exacting circumstances something that can be developed as part of one's consultancy skill? The AOC Programme Core Disciplines— consulting competence, organizational theory, and system psychodynamics, outlined earlier—provide conceptual and practical frameworks for engaging in change interventions with organizations in ways that have been illustrated here. Consultants have spoken about adjusting or repositioning themselves in the light of dominant mindsets (Davidson & Kinneen), entrepreneurial and market behaviours (Szlichcinski & Holder), and the turbulent dynamics of change itself (Owers; Van Linge). In these stories, mind-fulness emerges in waves of micro-narratives: local, temporary, provisional moments of paying attention that can be characterized in the tension between reliance on familiar modes and routines, and the novel ways in which these might come together to generate potential for change (Levinthal & Rerup, 2006).

Well-rehearsed routines and the construction of novel recombinations

A short story. A client whom I have worked with intermittently over the last ten years recently asked me to "come and do my usual thing" in running an experiential workshop for an inter-professional group. I challenged her on this, asking her to articulate what she thought characterized the usual thing that I did, and knowing that what might be usual for her might be entirely different for another client. She was able to say that she could expect me to create something imaginative and different, in the moment, with her particular group. It was a paradox of an engagement, holding both the usual and familiar in relation to how I might approach the task, and the different and strange in relation to what might emerge. It felt like pressure. Much as the invitation to do my usual thing in some respects felt like an enjoyable request, at another level I could feel the demand to create recognizable, yet innovative, outcomes.

I think this is not an unusual scenario: consultants are hired with multiple, often unspoken needs in mind (Grueneisen & Izod), but often with a hope that they will be able to achieve something novel in each engagement, based upon their previous successes. Consultants strive to build expertise in relation to their domains (Neumann, 2004), and inevitably come to prefer certain scenarios with which they feel familiar and competent. The pressure to speak to, or guarantee, outcomes is high, particularly where consultancy interventions are product orientated and must address return-on-investment formulae.

In the cases described here, consultants have not especially set out to bring novel solutions to their clients; rather, innovations have emerged as clients and consultants alike have supported the energy, or contained the risk, to engage in less bounded, freer interventions. Some trust in the capacity to recognize this point seems essential, while at a cognitive level Langer suggests that a break with routine can take on the quality of a "void" (Langer, 2005, p. 16), where similarities and differences can be recognized as complementarities, each having resonance in the other. The space offers the potential for noticing and attending to organizational cues in ways which can re-form or cluster anew, offering novel recombinations of previously familiar phenomena. Figure 1 represents how this might occur.

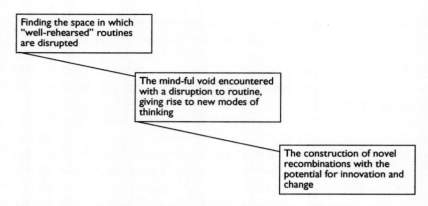

Figure 1. How creating a "void" can result in reformulating the familiar.

The use of narrative to encourage mind-fulness

Creating a break with routine will, for many consultants and client systems, be experienced as a challenge or threat to individual or organizational identity. The difficulties for an organization to hear feedback following an "identity" audit (Riise), or for the accountancy sector to take on a new mantle of ethical leadership (Dixon), indicate just how hard it is to give up the familiar and enduring and seek new dimensions.

In this section, I want to explore how the use of narrative structure might provide some containment in relation to identity, and also enable consultants to engage with more varied repertoires of intervention, so giving themselves and their client systems a greater potential for the kind of mind-ful attentiveness that has been outlined above.

Some narrative structures:

An epical and traditional storyline generally requires a central character, a plot, characters who relate to the key issues, and an outcome. Taking up a role in a narrative structure such as this requires a self-awareness and intention. It requires an attention to the "who am I?" in this storyline, where I begin and end: am I a narrator, a protagonist, a hidden player making a late appearance? In relation to these roles, some sense of plot needs to allow for an unfolding and escalation of events around people who populate these scenarios, and in relation to the issues they are facing. And, at some point, the story will conclude.

An epical storyline frequently will withhold part of the story, and will concern itself with external conflicts, often resolved through revelation, and through external events. Less traditional epical storylines provide revelations that are more internal, offering opportunities to revisit what has gone before and perceive it in a new light. Lyrical storylines highlight technique and style over the plot and characterization, often rearranging dimensions of sequence and dialogue. They are developed through sustained imagery, working as a motif against which plots and actions can be viewed, and capable ultimately of transformation. They tend to avoid endings that offer complete resolution, and are more open and suggestive. An "artifice" storyline introduces two seemingly different and unconnected streams, which must find ultimate meaning in each other, and which challenge previous perceptions and shape those to come. (For more information on these narrative structures, see www.commapress.co.uk.)

Crafting a storyline where we may be in at least some control of our characters and their destinies is inevitably a different proposition to inhabiting lived roles in complex organizations, with outcomes that are often unpredictable. However, I want to propose that, as consultants, we can improve our intervention choices by attending to where we might take a break from our preferred identities, where we might access different modes of thinking, and thereby reconfigure how we intervene—putting together a different kind of wardrobe, as Whittle suggests in her introduction.

Working with narrative structure, then, might include making parallel choices about what is set out in Table 1.

For some consultants, working out "who I am" has been pivotal to their capacities to attend to what is happening in the moment, and consequently to increase their repertoires to engage in the client's storyline. Walsh & Whittle, Davidson & Kinneen, and Grueneisen & Izod have all created ways of exploring their identities as consultants, showing how earlier mindsets, or experiences, have been brought into the present in ways that have held them to limiting positions. With role encompassing both inner-world associations and external world requirements on task and behaviour, it

Table 1.   The process of choosing a narrative structure.

Storyline	Consultant repertoire
Who am I in the narrative?	Who am I as the consultant/manager?
What is the plot?	How do I perceive the client system?
How does the plot develop in relation to its characters and their issues, and how does the literary form support that (i.e., is technique figural or ground)?	How is change encountered, and how can I intervene in relation to complex micro-narratives?
What kind of storyline am I in, and how does it influence outcome?	What kind of outcomes are recognizable, valued, and possible?

has been necessary at points to give up aspects of their preferred selves—as peers, as essentially collaborative, and to make space for new configuration—that might open themselves up to dynamics of competition, power, and vulnerability in their relations.

Focusing on how the client system (or the plot) is constructed has been at the foreground of chapters by Nardone, Johnson, & Vitulano, and Szlichcinski and Holder. Here, attention has focused on the situations that the client inhabits, the nature of characters involved, and their dilemmas and complexities emerging over time. Responding to those client scenarios has encouraged changes to preferred consultancy styles, in the construction of specific teams and partnerships, as a move away from working individually. These have posed their own opportunities and demands, as well as disruption to a more usual mode of practice. A feature has been the growing sector and organizational knowledge that these consultants have had to incorporate into their practice, the extent to which they can be both knowing and unknowing, as they build up specific expertise over time, yet come new to each specific client.

Interventions that have focused on the nature of change over time (or the dimensions of the plot) have found compelling imagery, both at the heart of their interventions and driving them. This is seen in the vivid illustrative motifs of energy through which Dixon has sought to access a more ethical stance in professional behaviour. Similarly, Owers' spirals, vortices, and turbulent flows provide rich associative media through which organizational actors find new ways to make sense of their world, and gain new repertoires with which they can move the organization forward. Riise's motifs of identity, brand, and reputation derive from powerful imagery of the way that things are done in the cultural life of the organization. Ambivalence about these motifs leads to an unknown future, the story cannot find an ending, and there is constant agitation. These are lyrical storylines, where technique and the power of the image are at the forefront, holding in themselves the capacity for new perspectives (revelations) to come about in surprising and energizing ways.

The artifice of bounded instability (van Linge) speaks to the tension of two apparently separate and unconnected features of the plot, the need for sufficient stability and containment to manage change, and the need for sufficient instability to provide the impetus. These kinds of consulting dilemmas, which frequently present themselves as polarities, here are held as complementarities, each containing the kernel of the one in the other. Here, the tension of holding these in relation to each other creates a need to reconfigure the consultancy role, at least in the mind, working between different repertoires of facilitation, process consultation, and leadership expert.

Sama's description of the historical narrative, and the organization that needs to find ways to relate to its past, but also to let it go to enable new organization structures and roles to emerge, provides us with the meta-narrative. This is the story of the story, the challenge to be in the present, to let go of previously held ideals, to create space in the minds, and to reformulate with intention.

To conclude

These chapters, with their micro-narratives, their attention to complexity, their focus on being present, speak to a meta-narrative of mind-fulness in the way that consultants go about practising their craft. I have suggested that using a narrative structure can help consultants to identify where they are in their engagements with their clients, what they are focusing on, and what potential that might offer for relinquishing or re-engaging with other parts of the storyline. In other words, to work, where possible, with a choice about who one is, the intervention repertoire that is available, and the nature of learning that is possible, all have the potential to increase one's own agency in the engagement and develop a capacity for mind-fulness.

References

Germer, C. (2005). Mindfulness. What is it? What does it matter? In: C. K. Germer, R. D. Siegel, & P. R. Fulton (Eds.), *Mindfulness and Psychotherapy* (pp. 3–27). New York: Guilford.

Langer, E. (2005). *On Becoming an Artist: Reinventing Yourself Through Mindful Creativity*. New York: Ballantine.

Levinthal, D., & Rerup, C. (2006). Crossing an apparent chasm: bridging mindful and less-mindful perspectives on organizational learning. *Organization Science, 17*(4): 502–513.

Neumann, J. E. (2004). Reforming consultancy identity in relation to discontinuities with clients. Paper presented to Academy of Management Annual Meeting, New Orleans, Louisiana, August.

INDEX

The inter connected of
complexity that
relate to too many
interdependancy
not ignoring the more

CWN
admin@citywomen.org

The painfulness of
imposed change
is the crack
open up beneath yr feet

Vincent.
Vincent.Traynor@bt.com